Our animal friends play a vital role in the balance of nature.
They help maintain the diversity and beauty of our world. However, for a
variety of reasons, some of them are facing serious threats that put them
in danger.

It is the responsibility of all of us to protect these incredible beings.
We can make a difference by adopting sustainable practices, such as
saving energy, recycling and respecting animals' natural habitats.
Plus, we can learn more about endangered species and support
organizations working to save them.

Let's be guardians of our planet, taking care of animals and the
environment. Together, we can ensure that future generations can also
appreciate the wonder of wildlife.

Rozana Sarmanho
2024

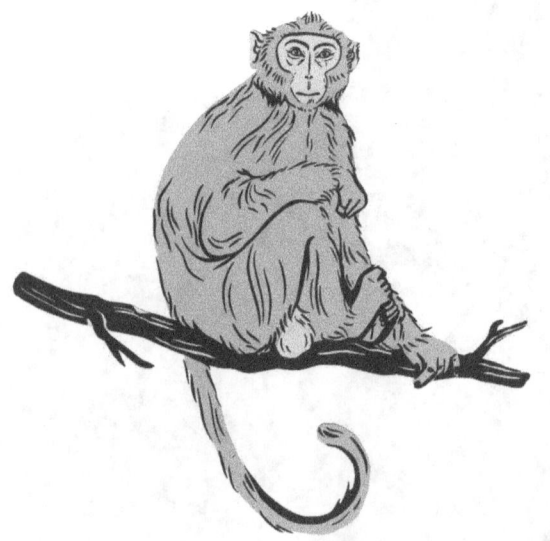

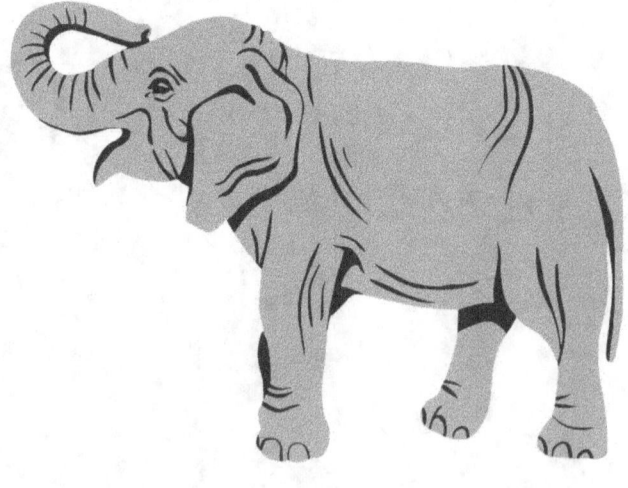

This Book Belongs to:

◇⋯⋯⋯⋯⋯⋯⋯⋯⋯⋯⋯⋯⋯⋯⋯◇

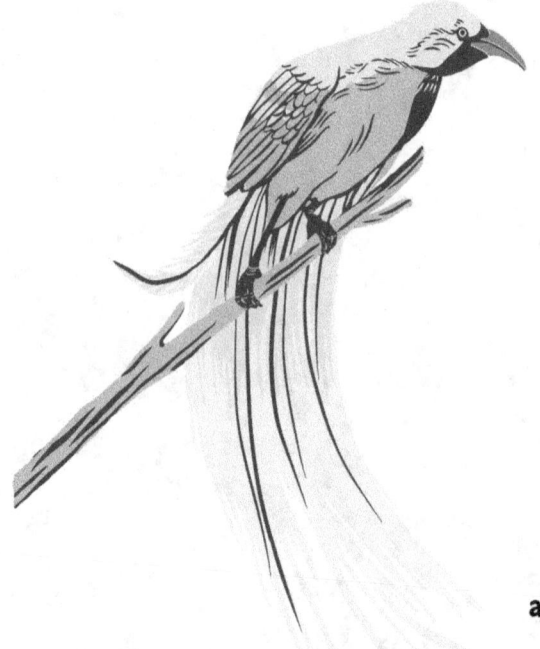

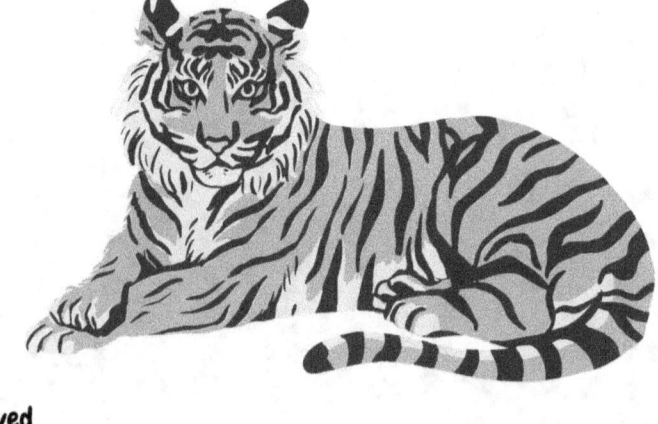

Test Color Page

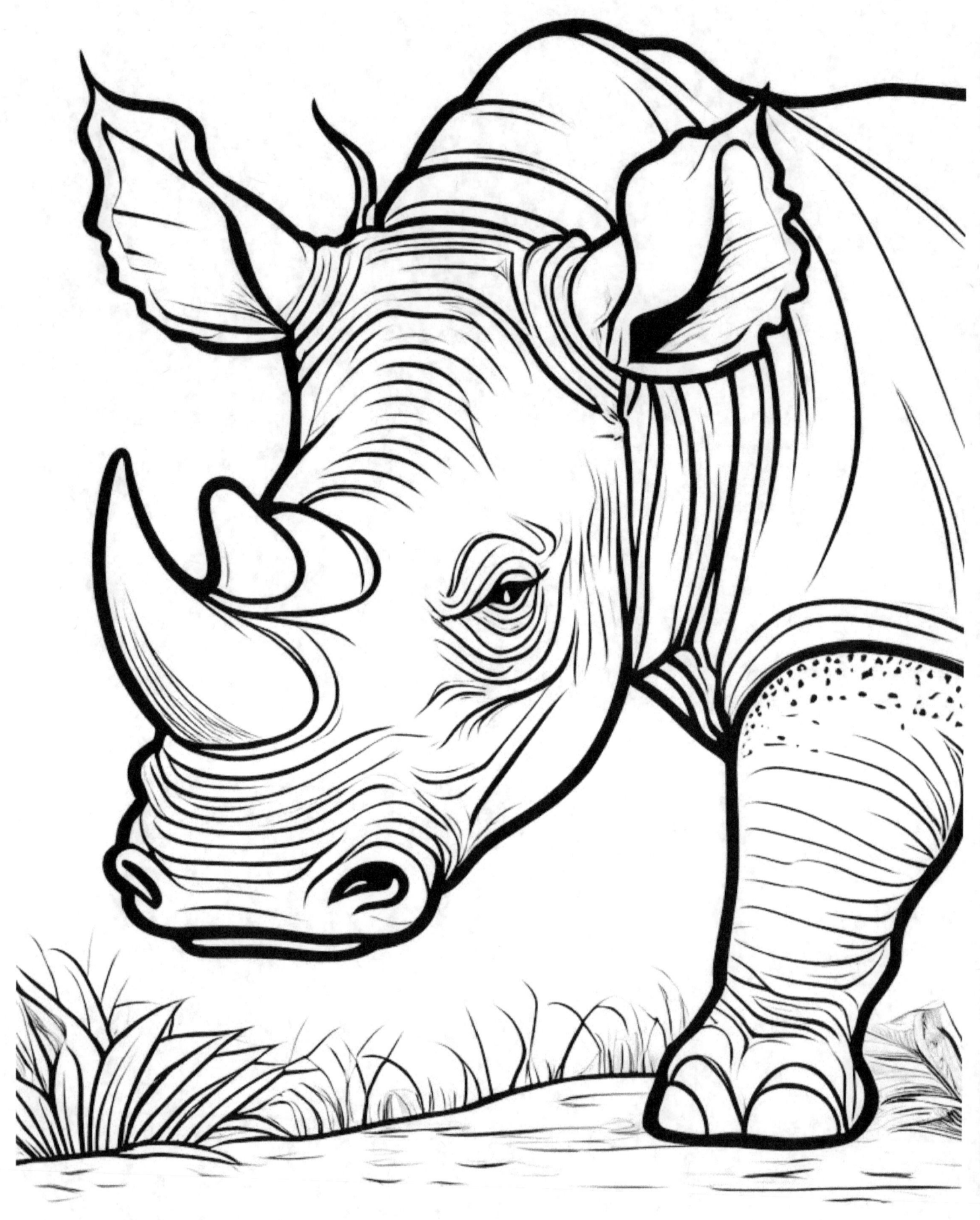

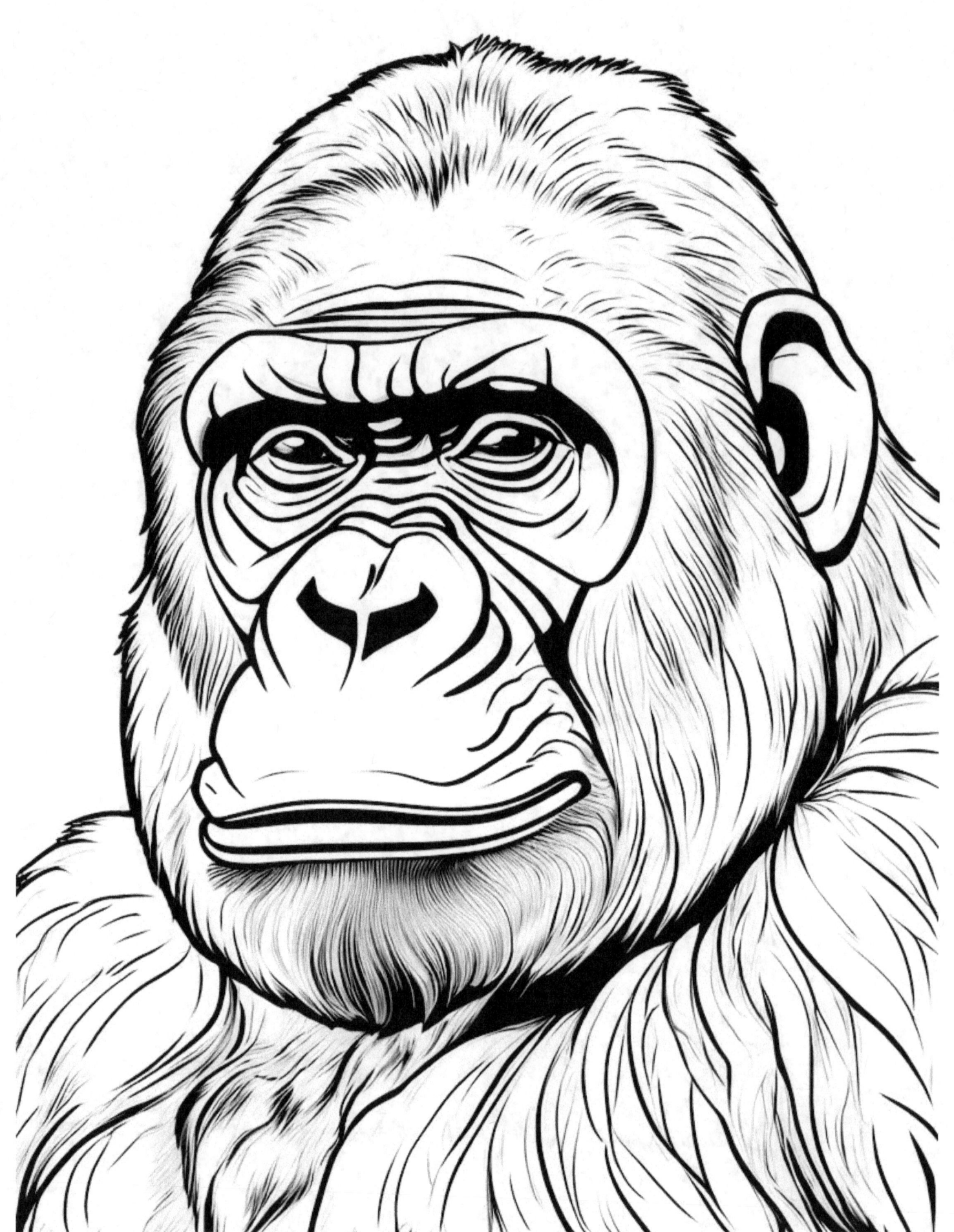

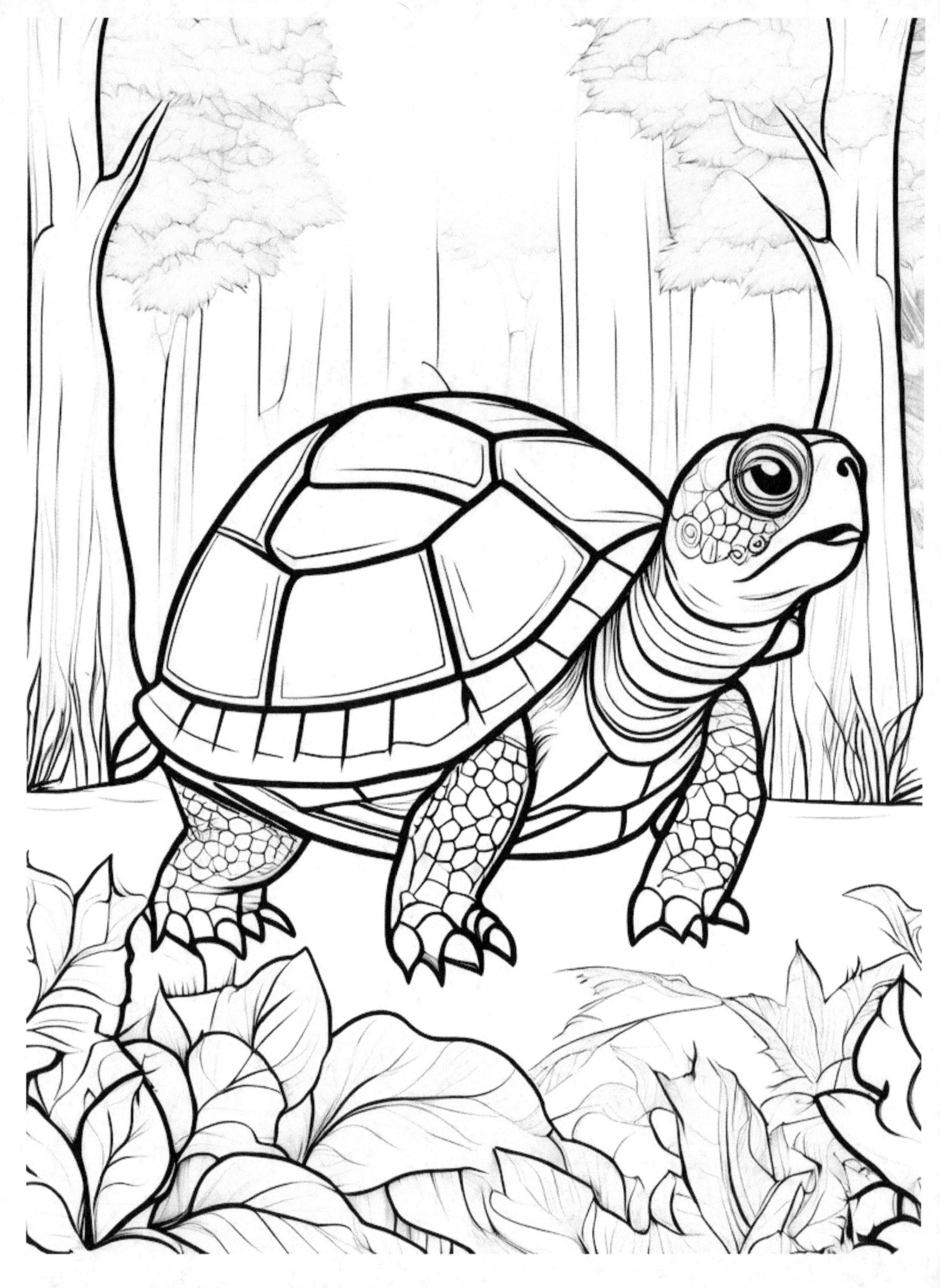

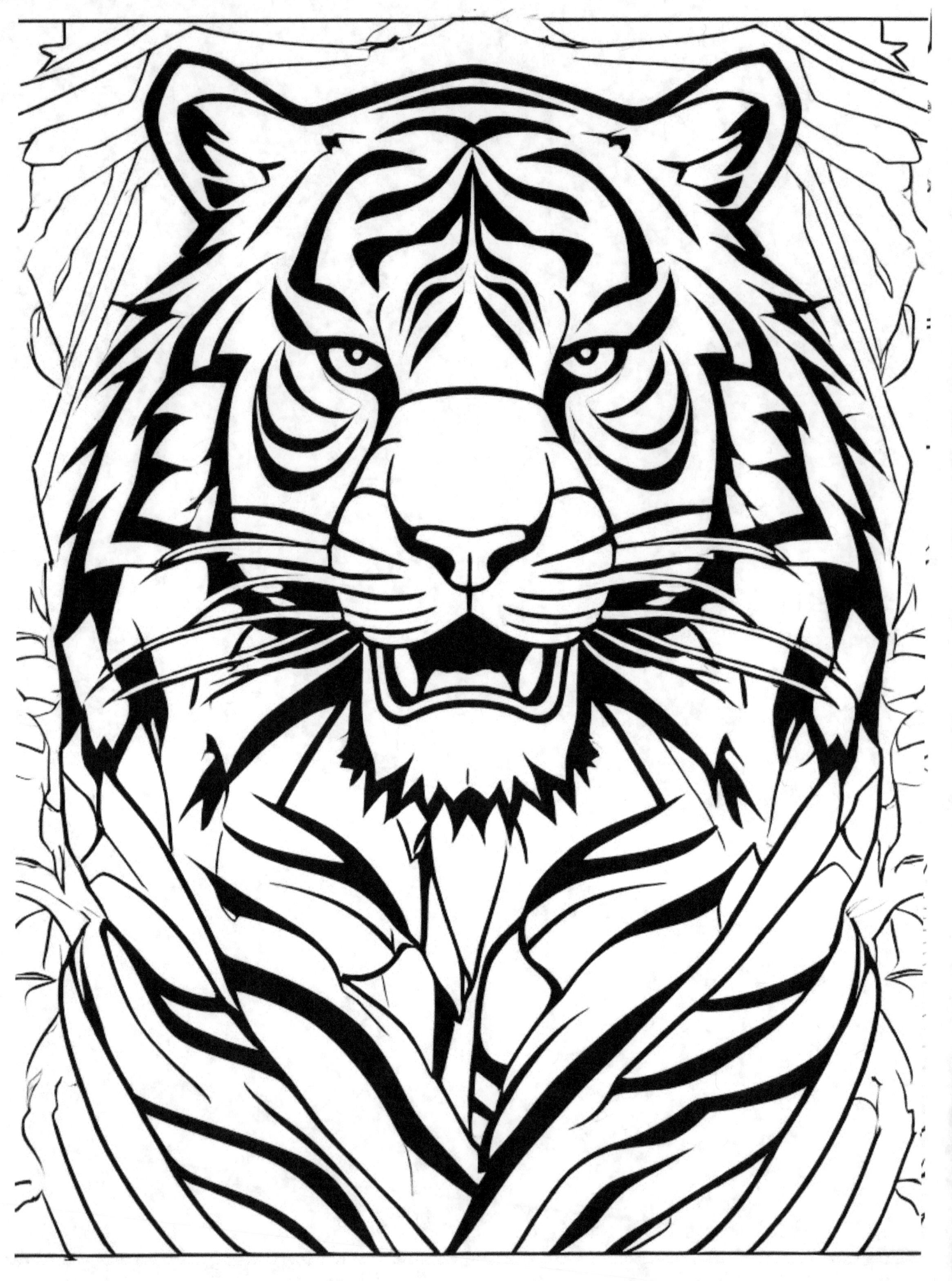

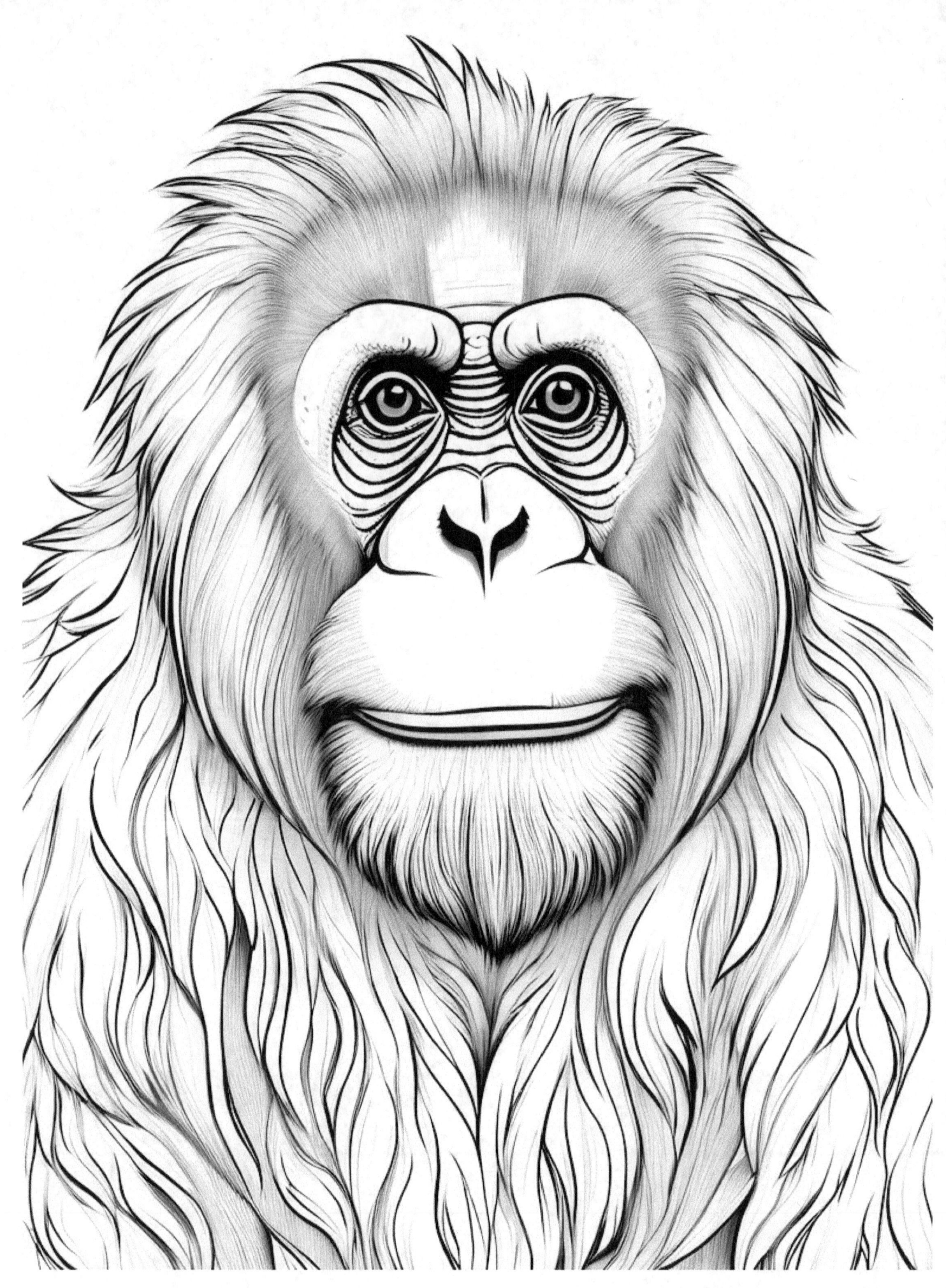

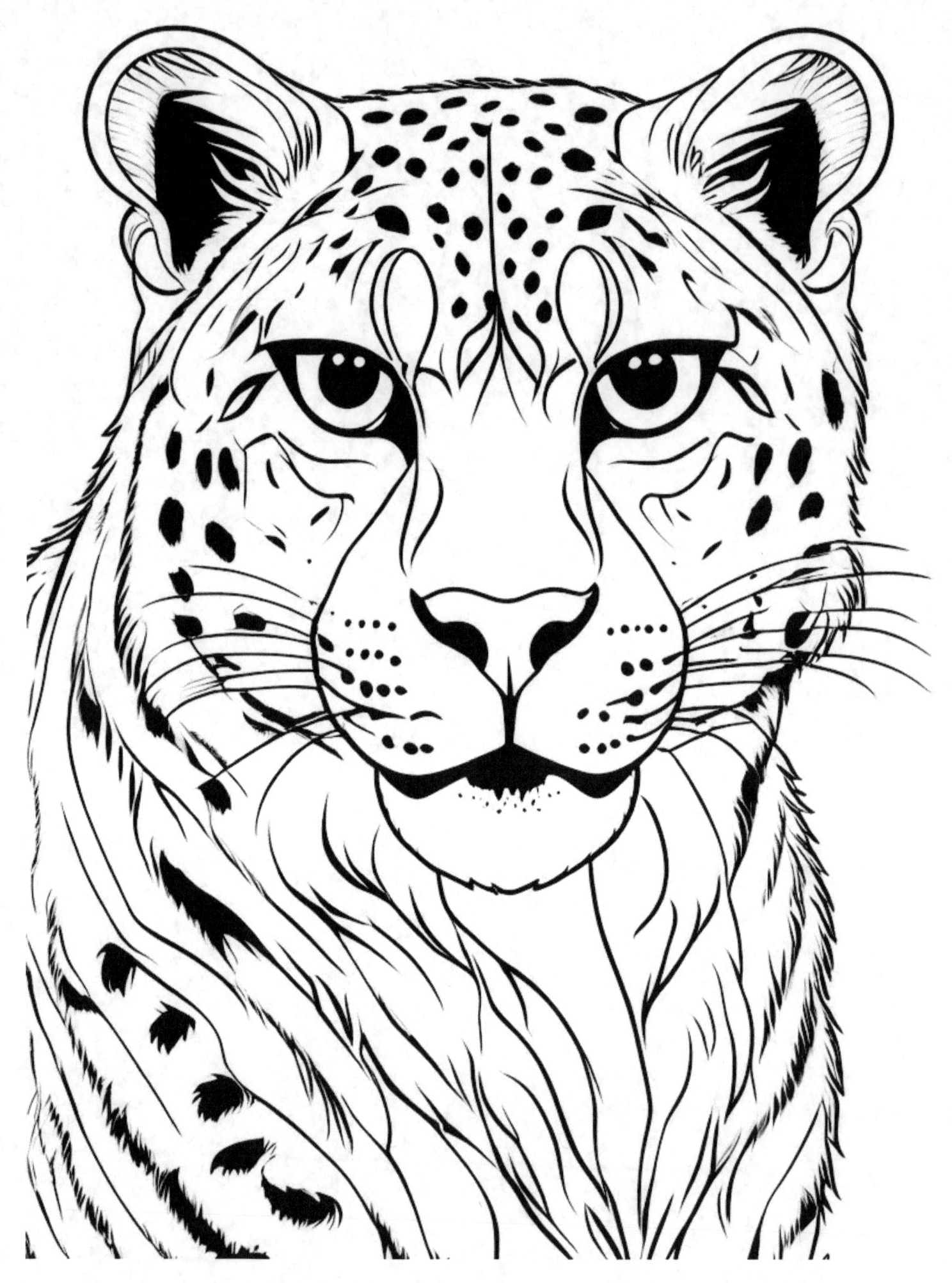

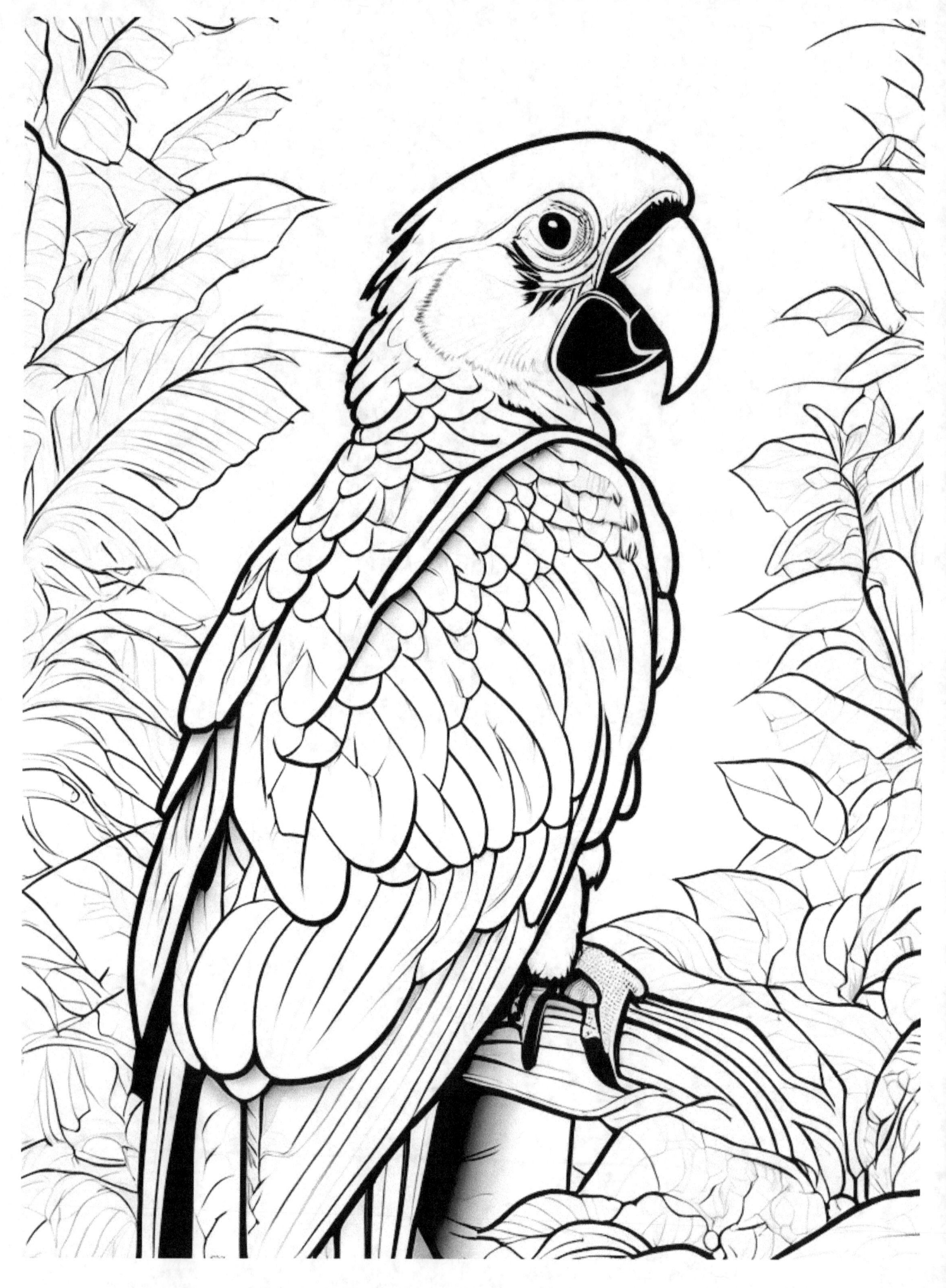

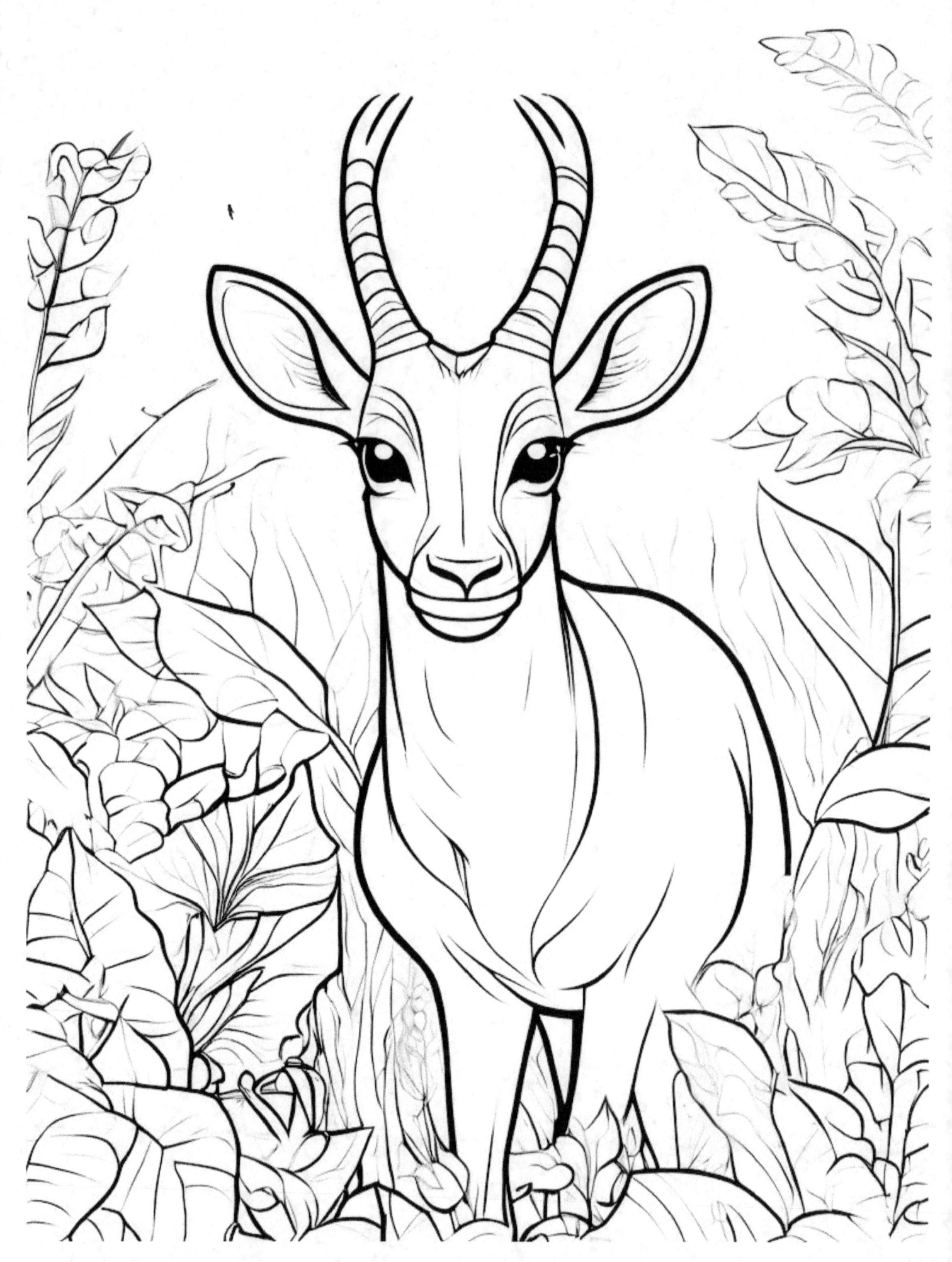

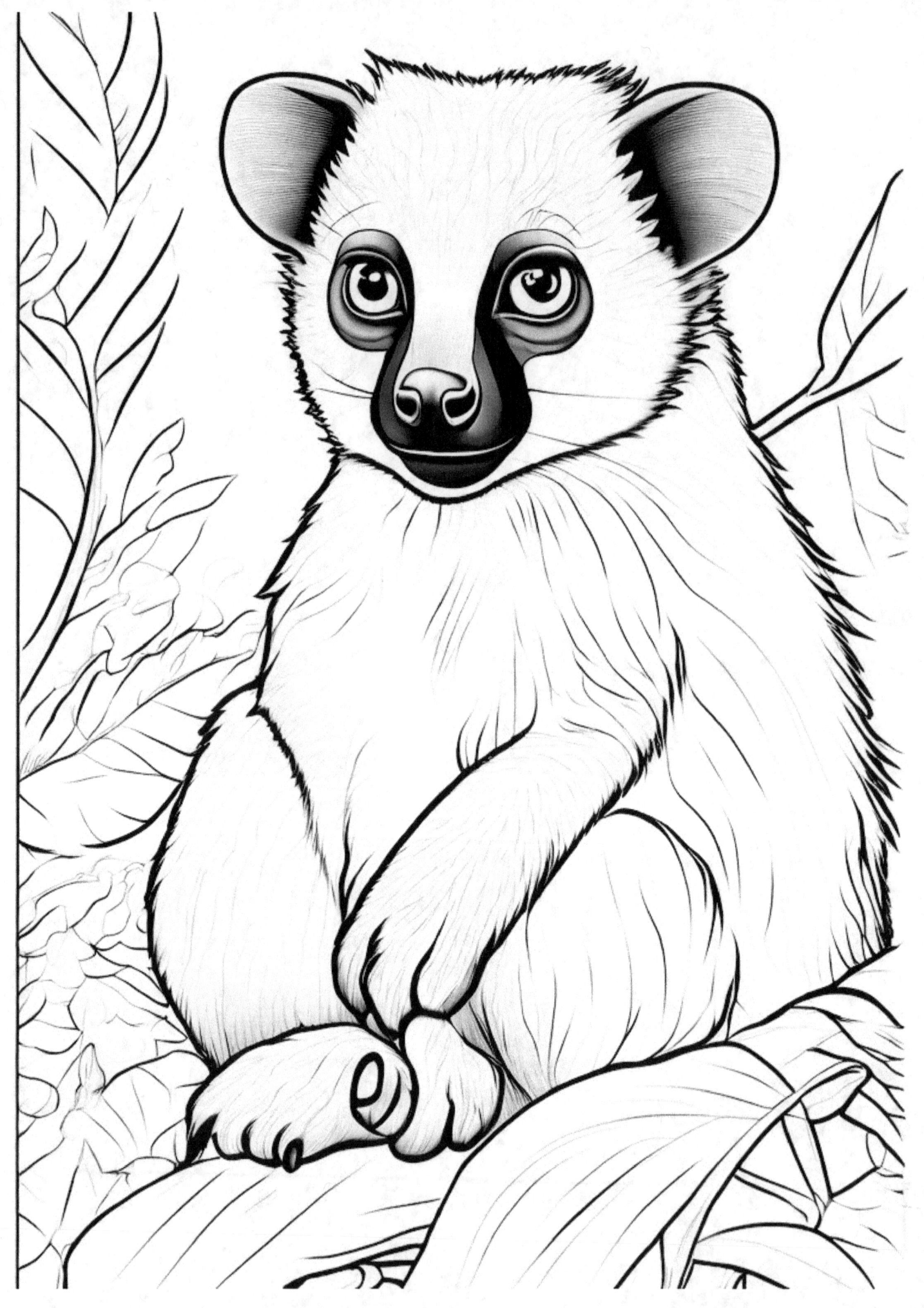

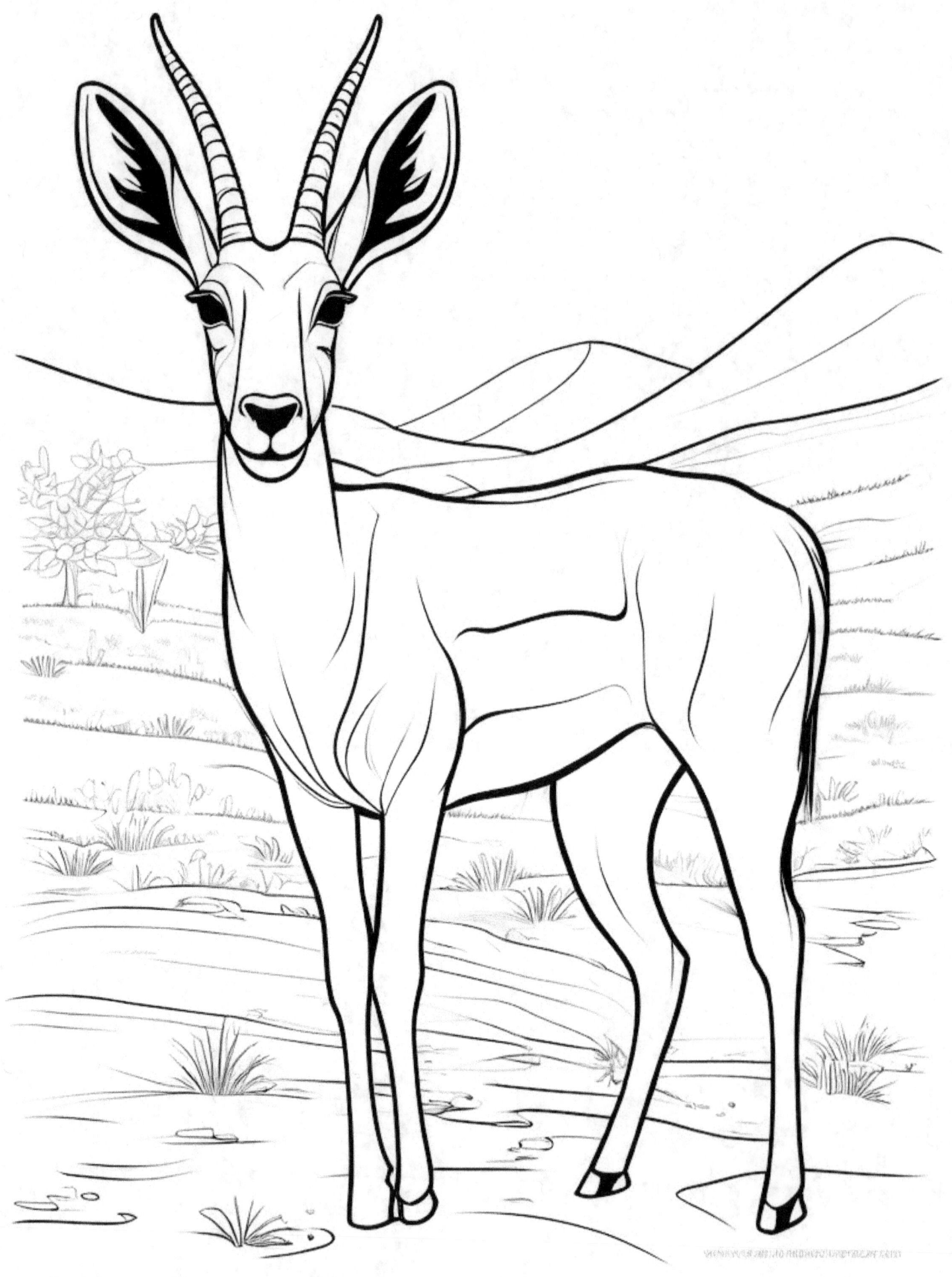

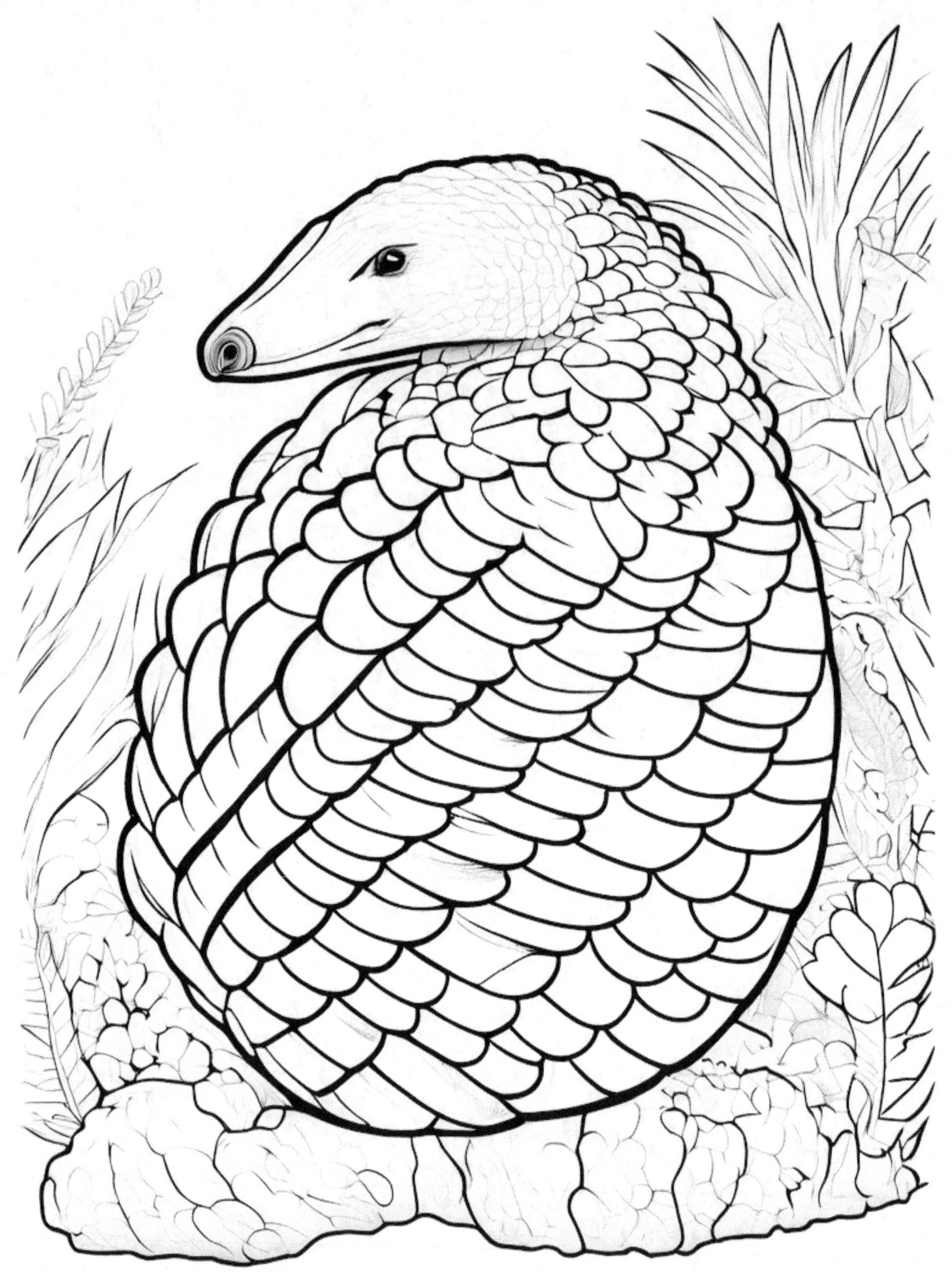

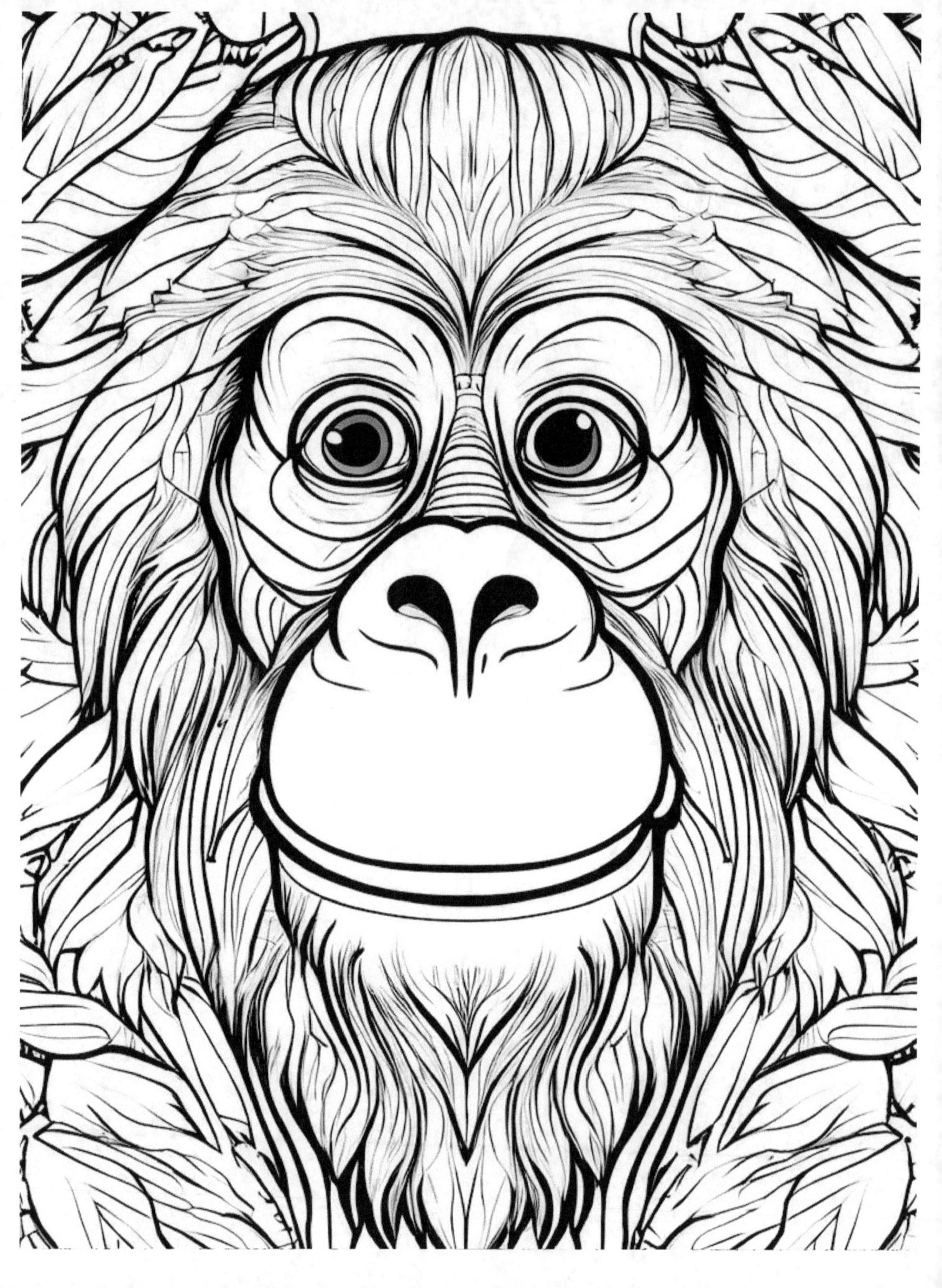

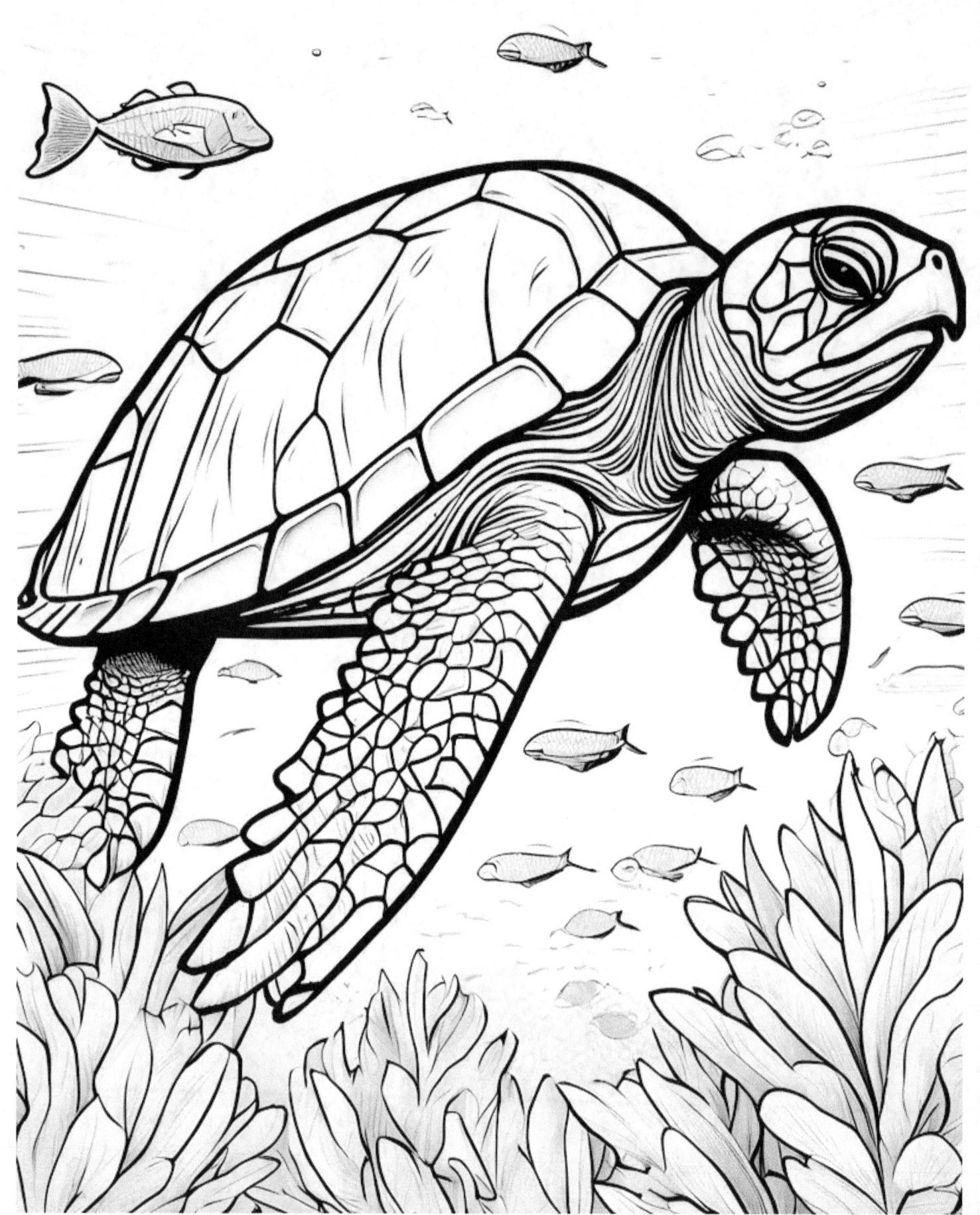

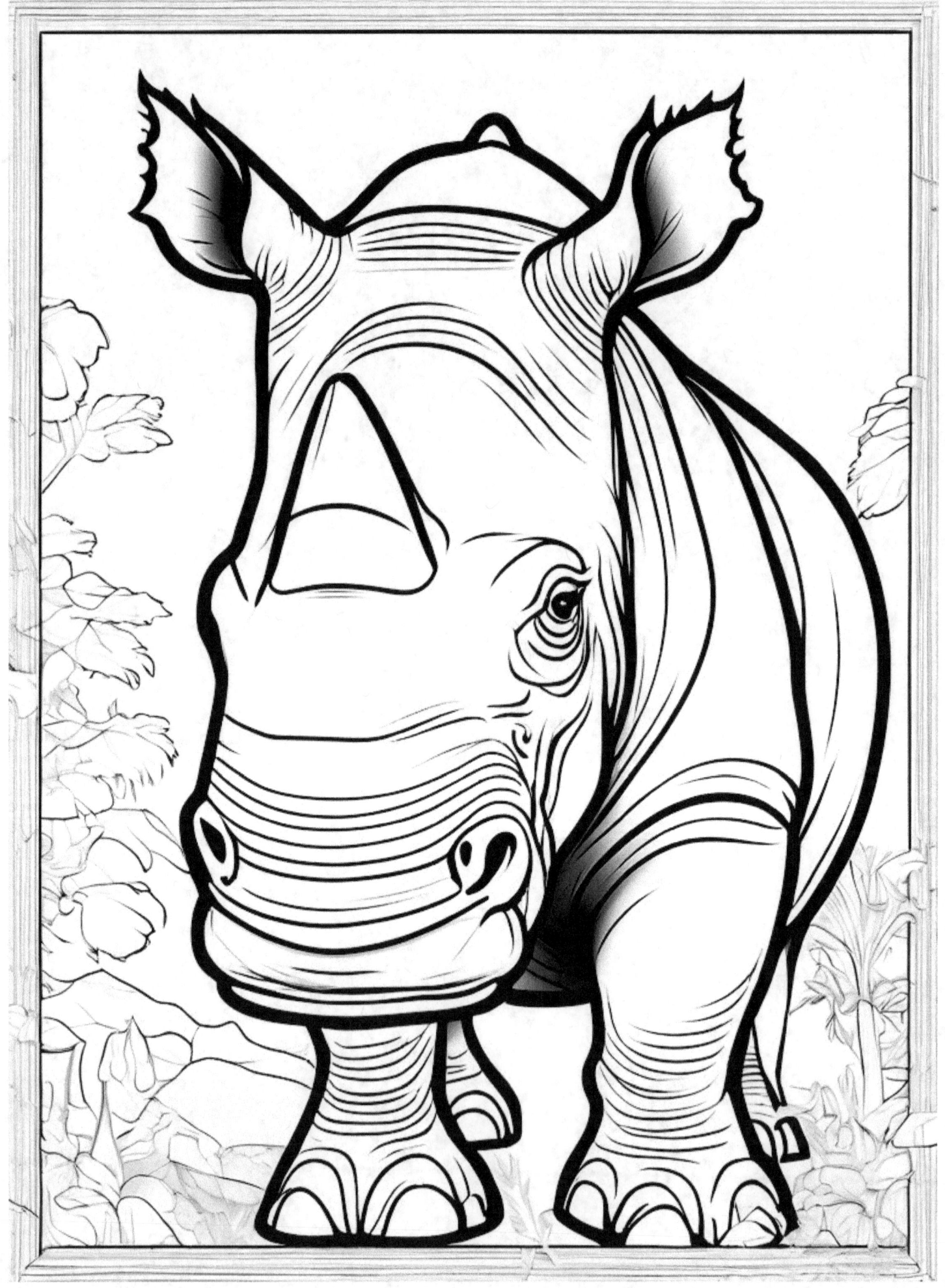

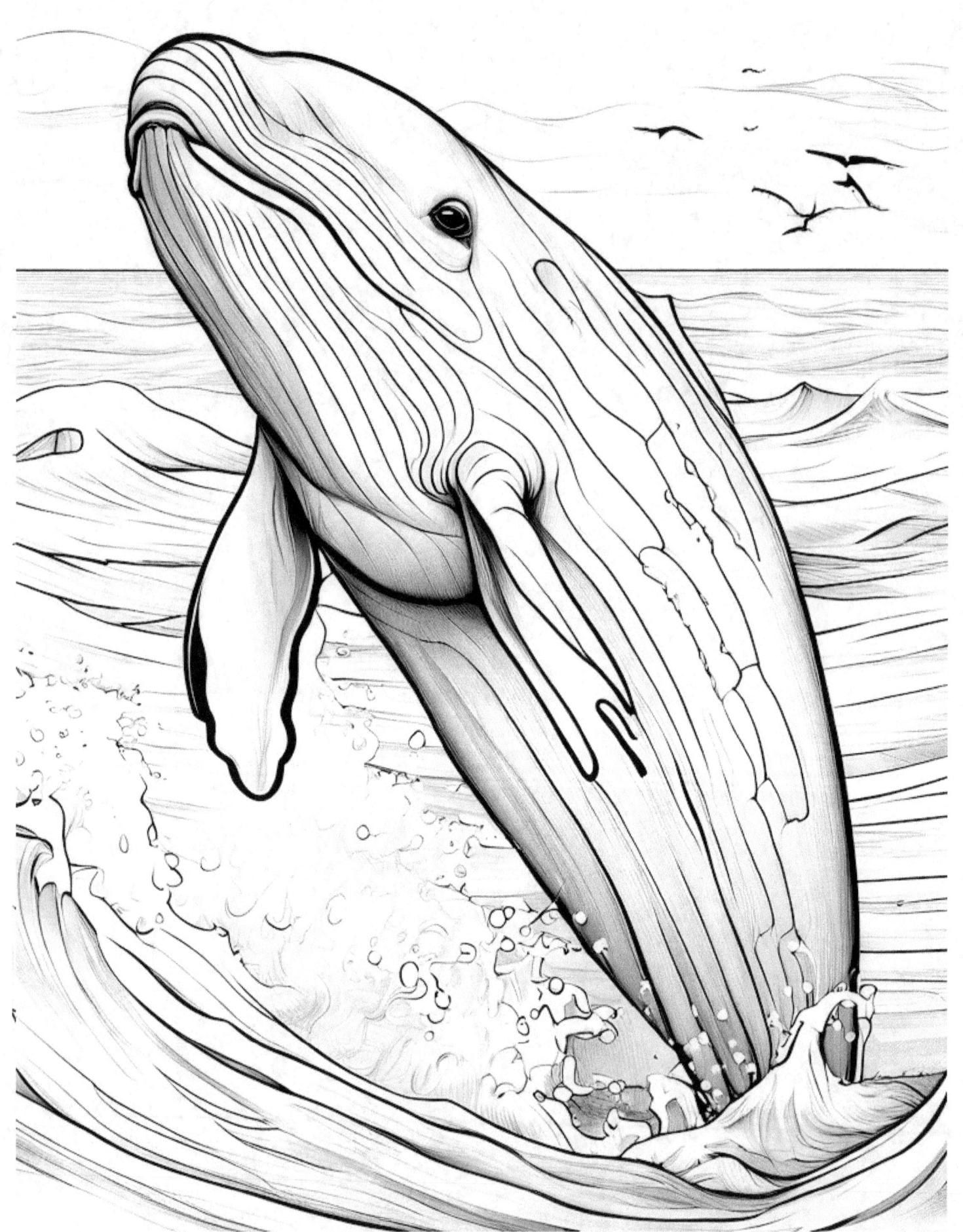

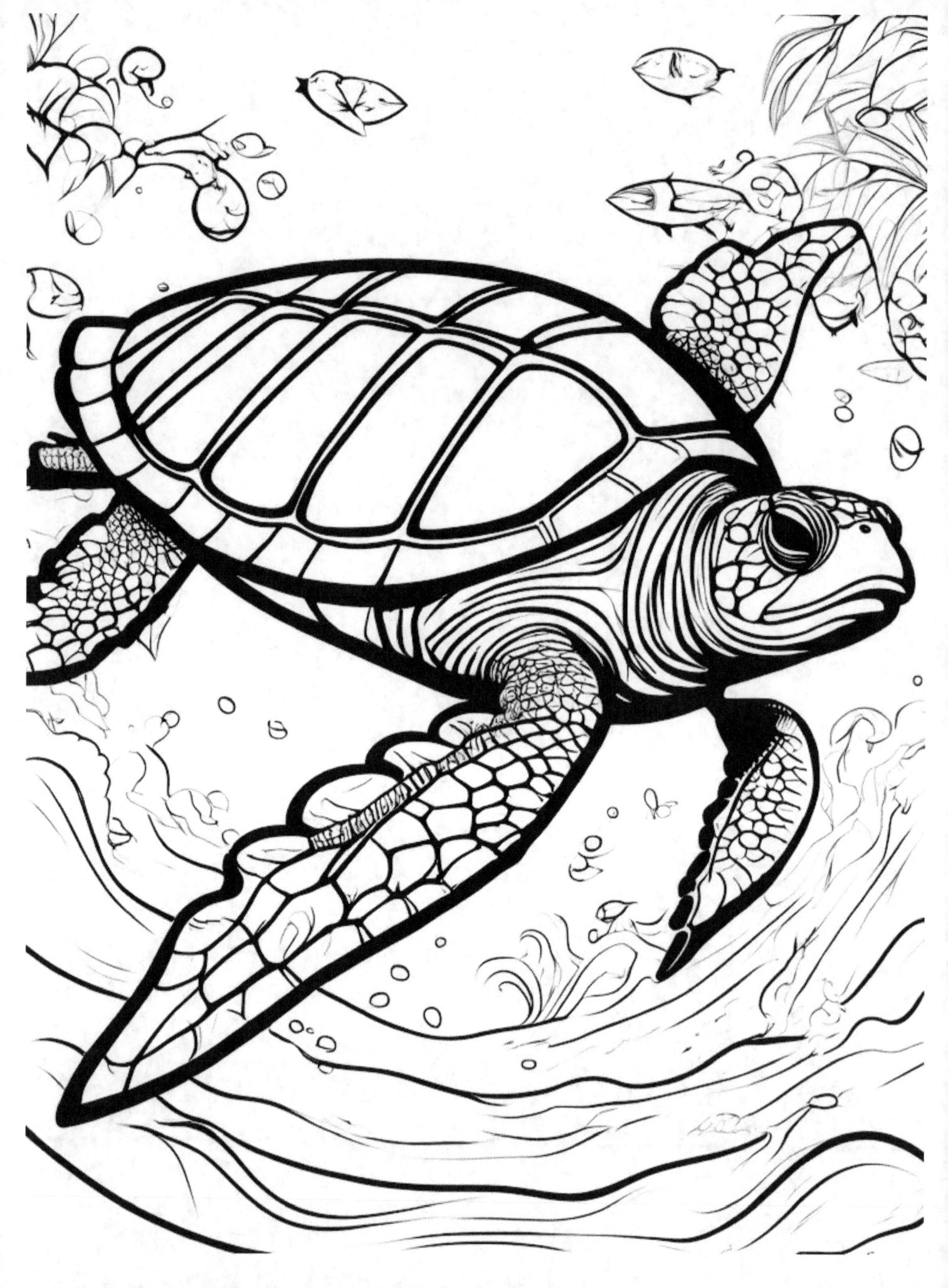

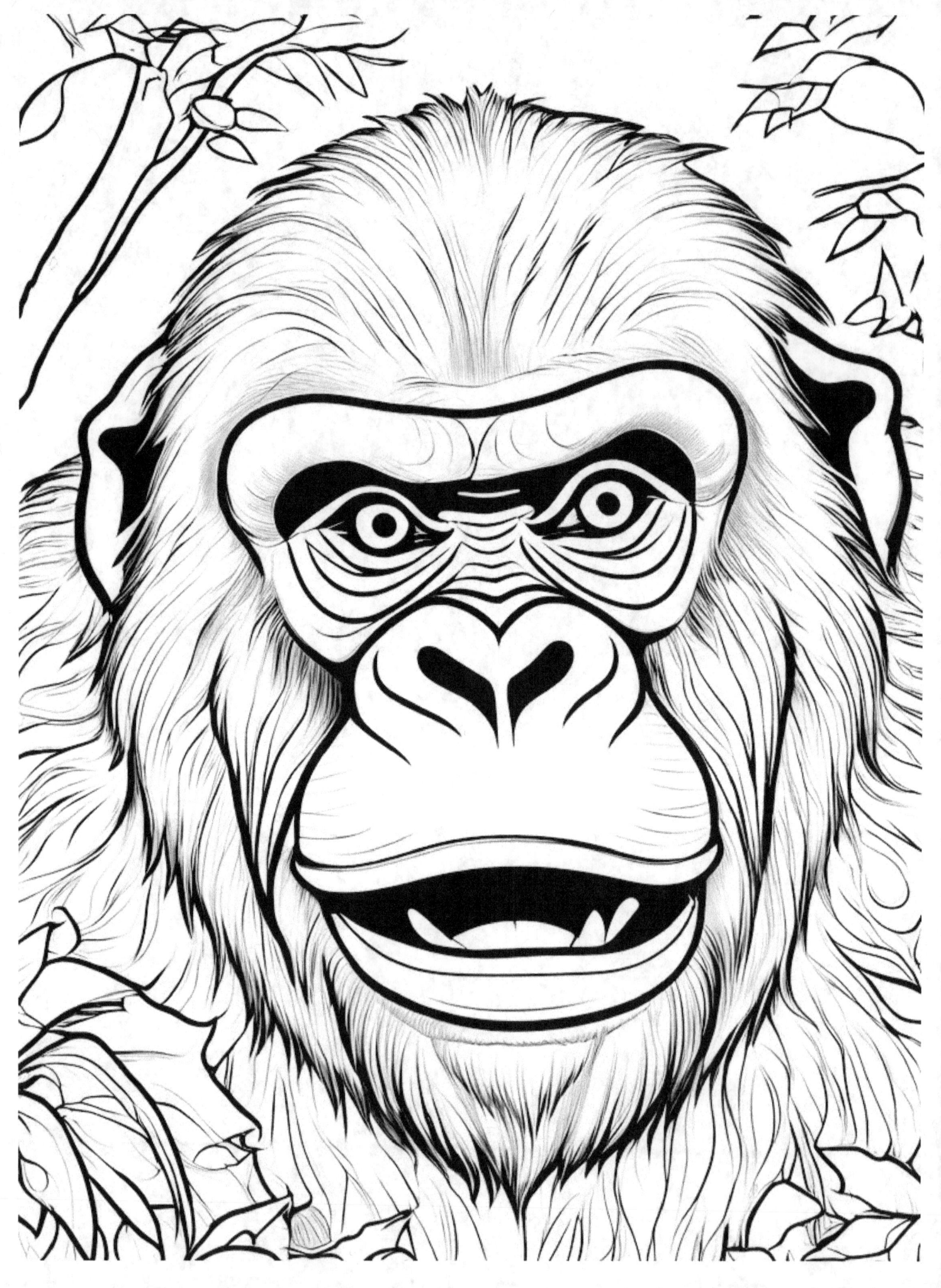

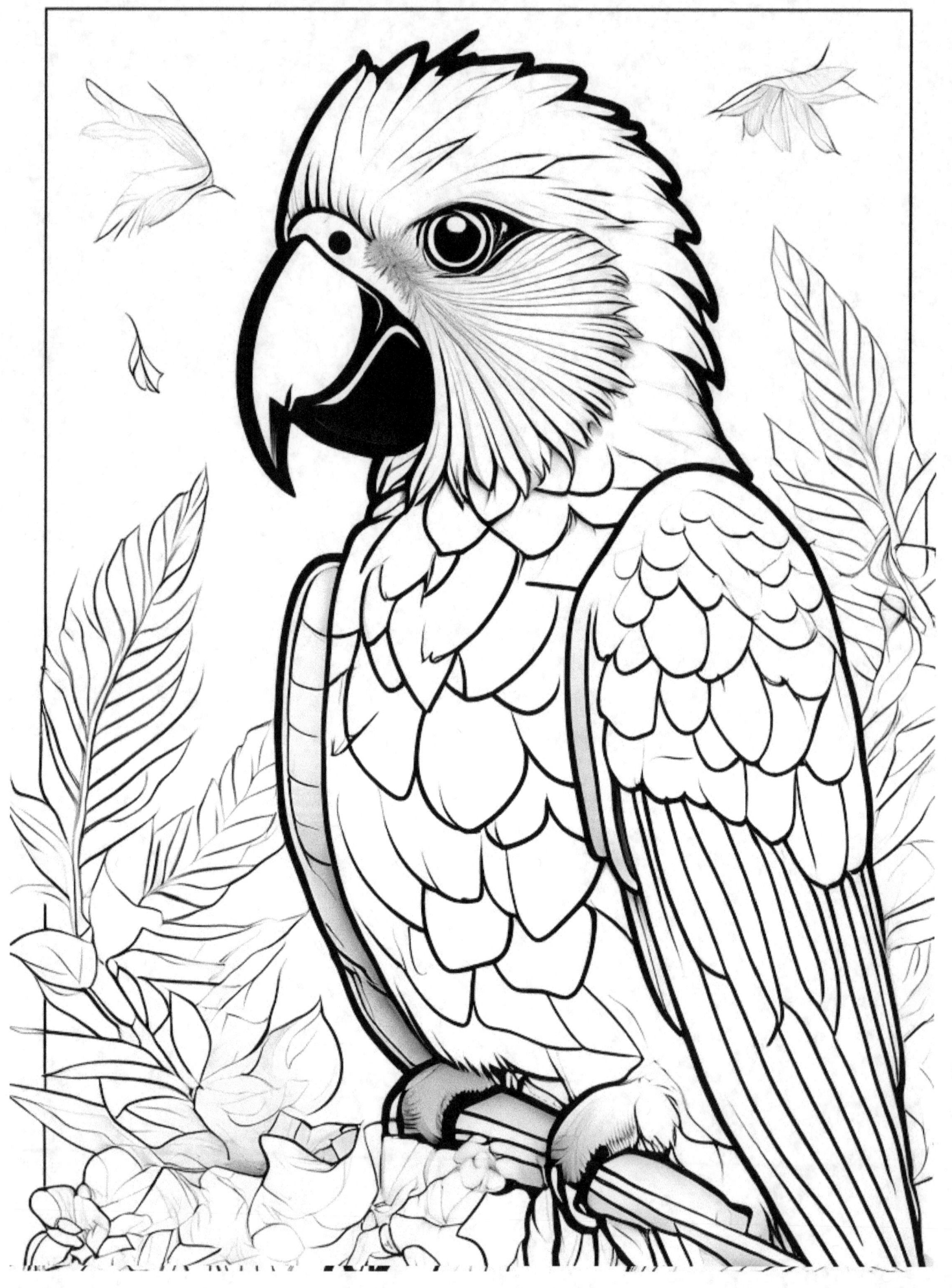

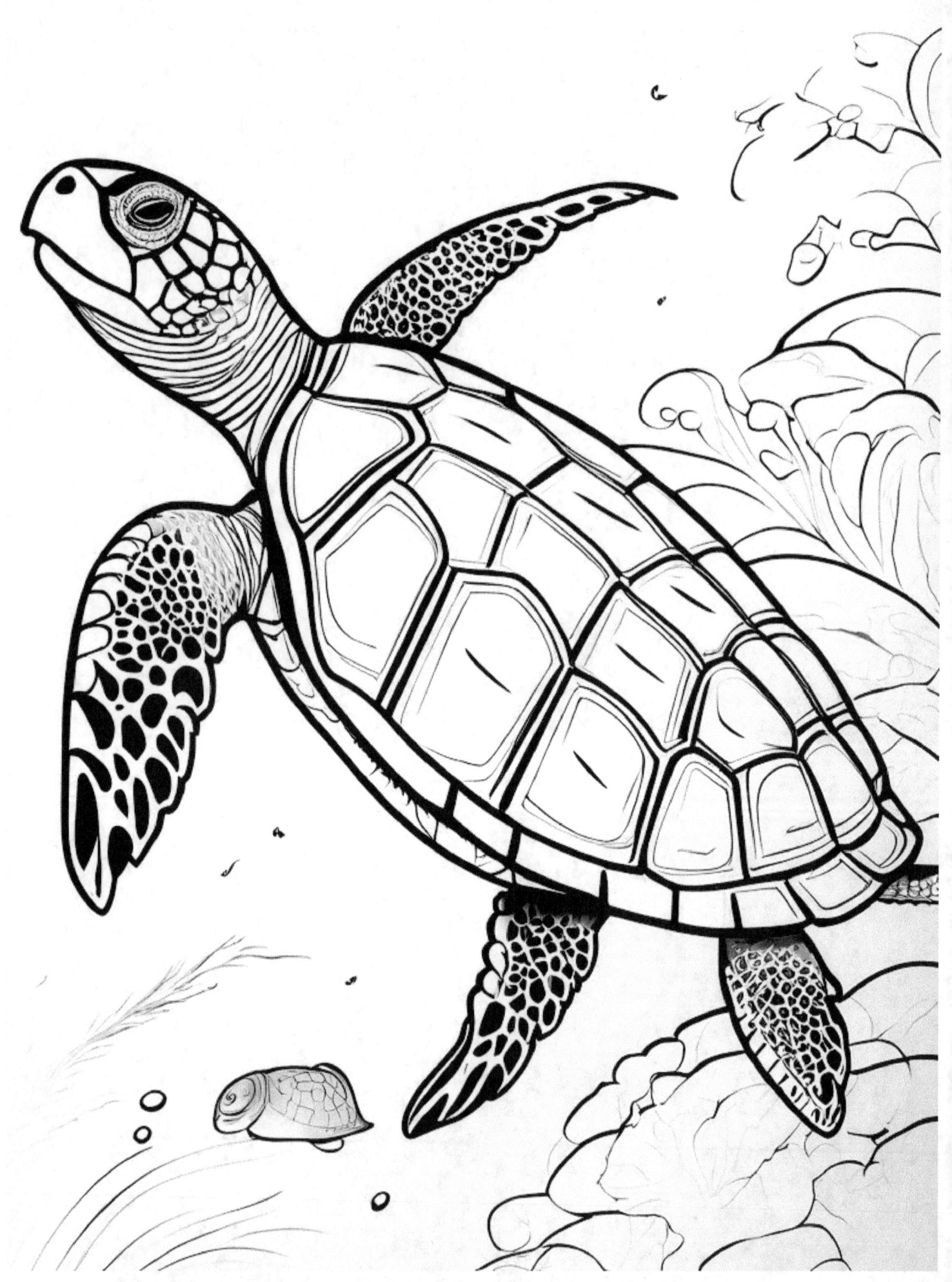

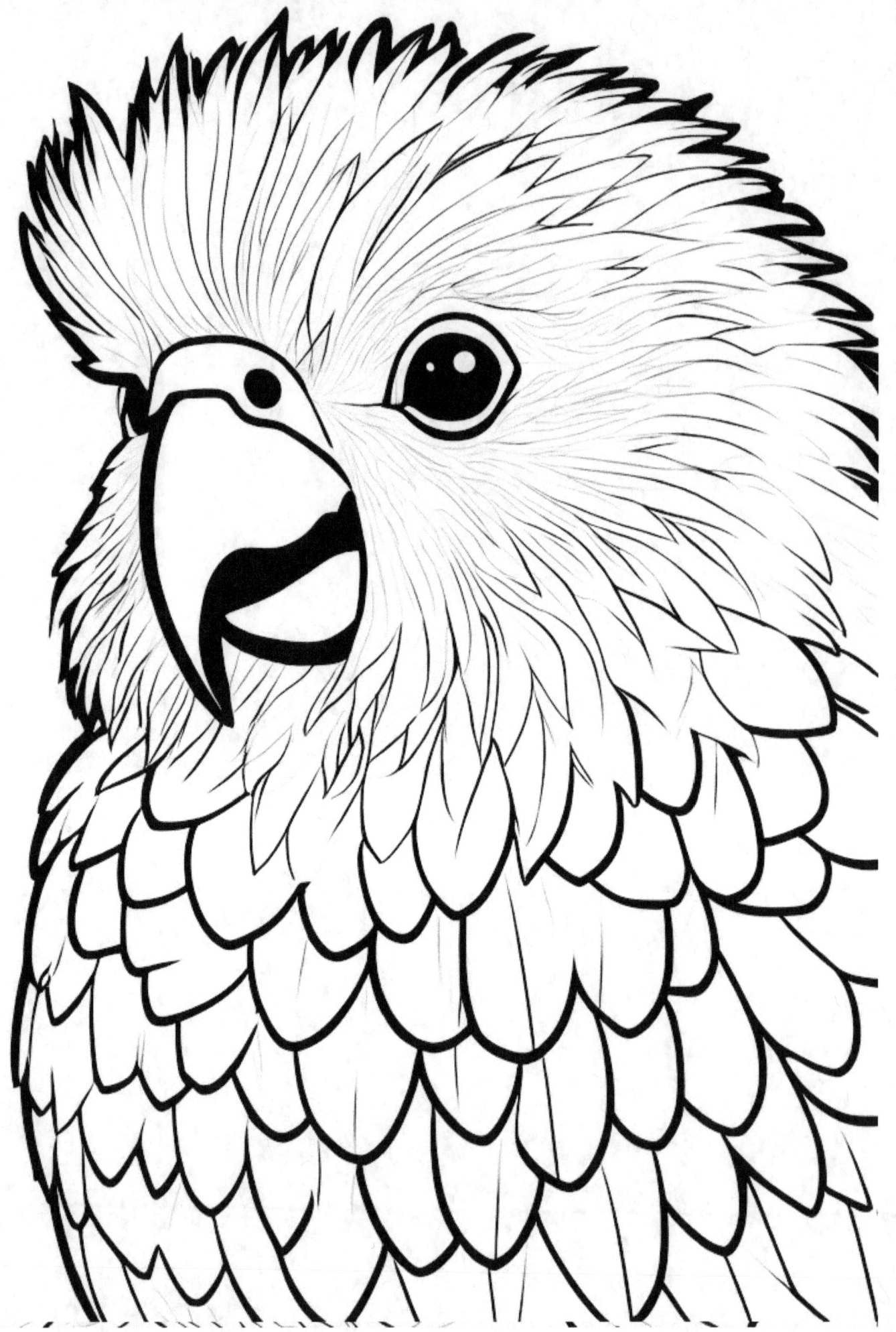

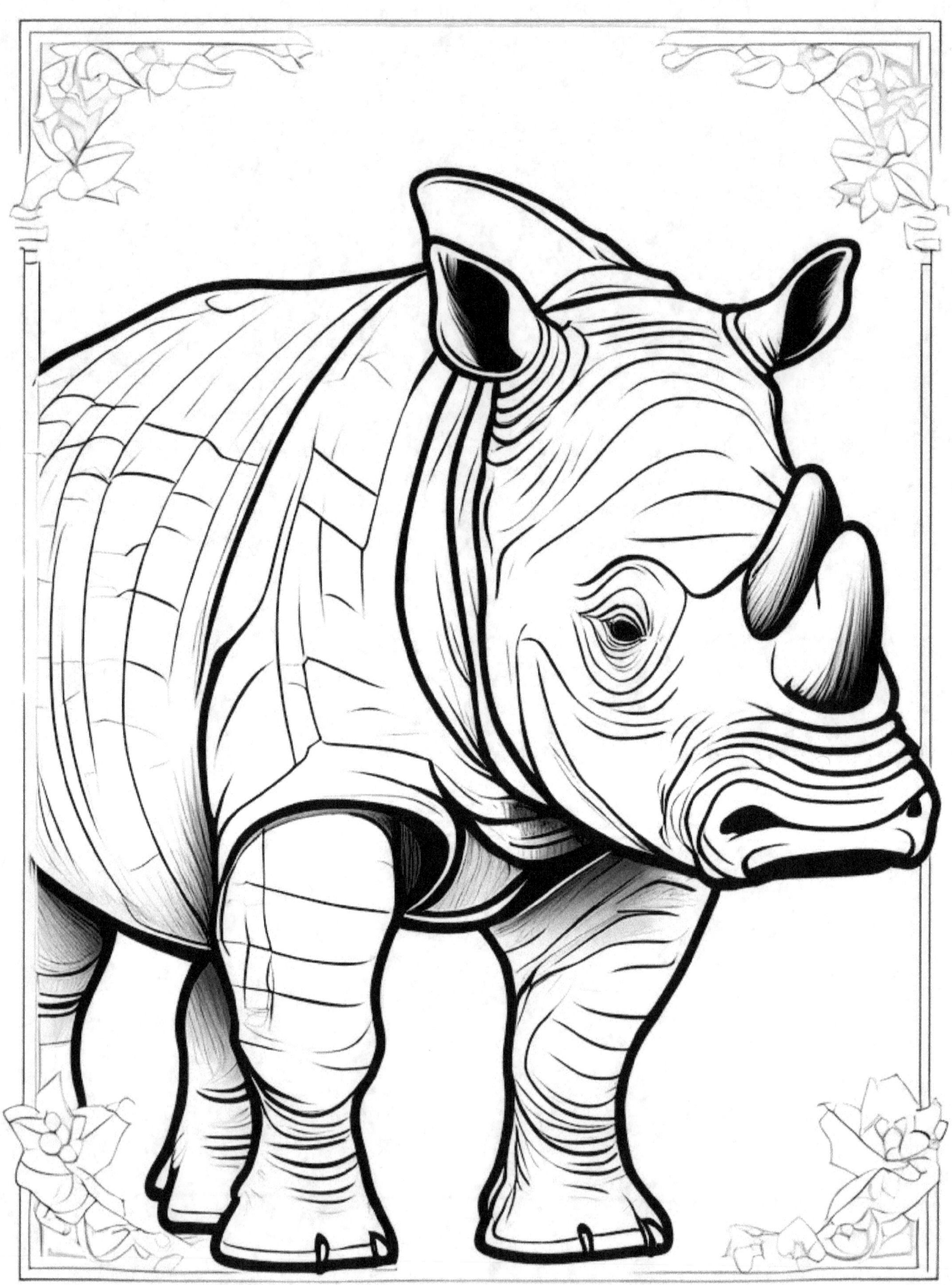

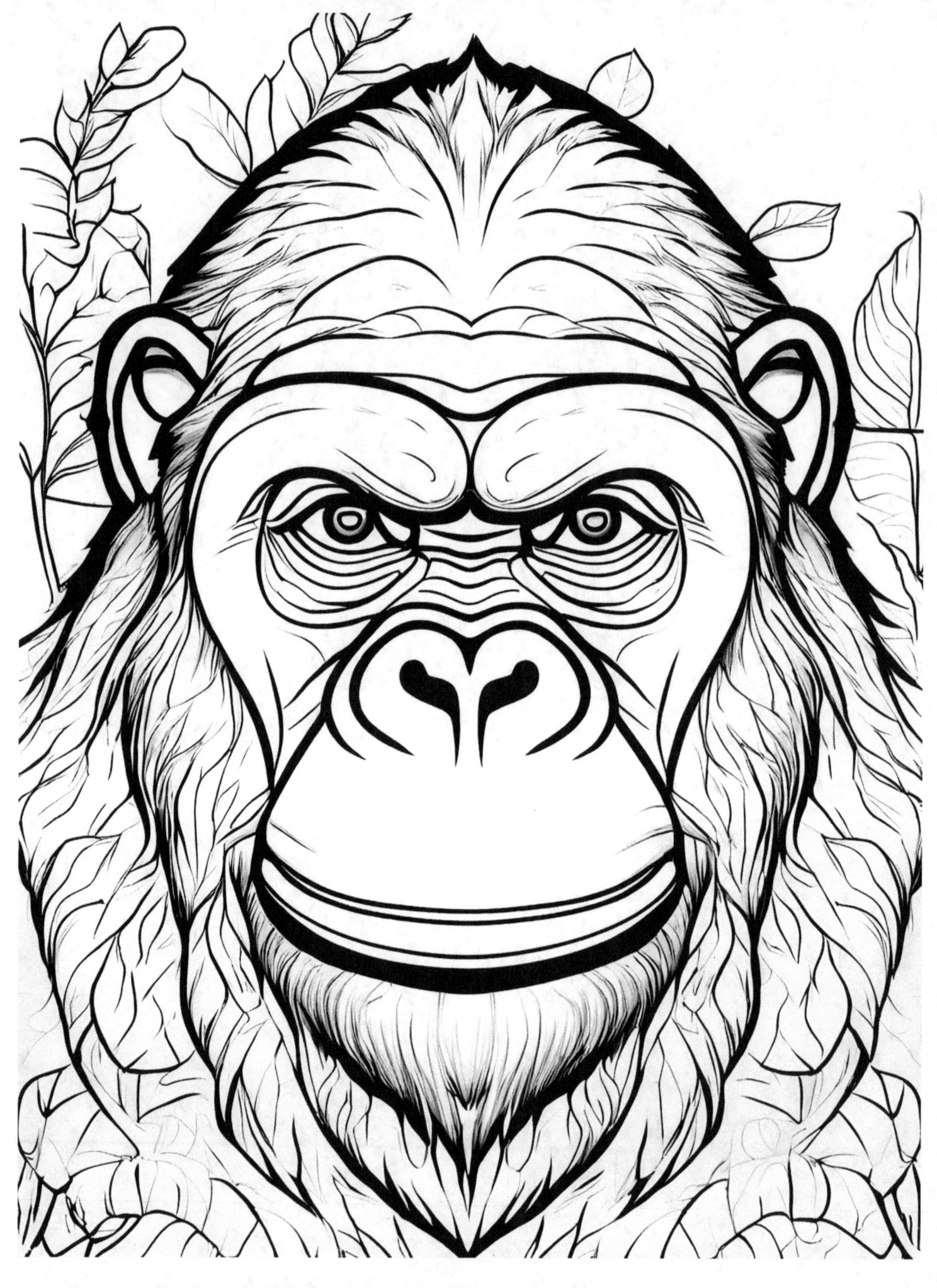

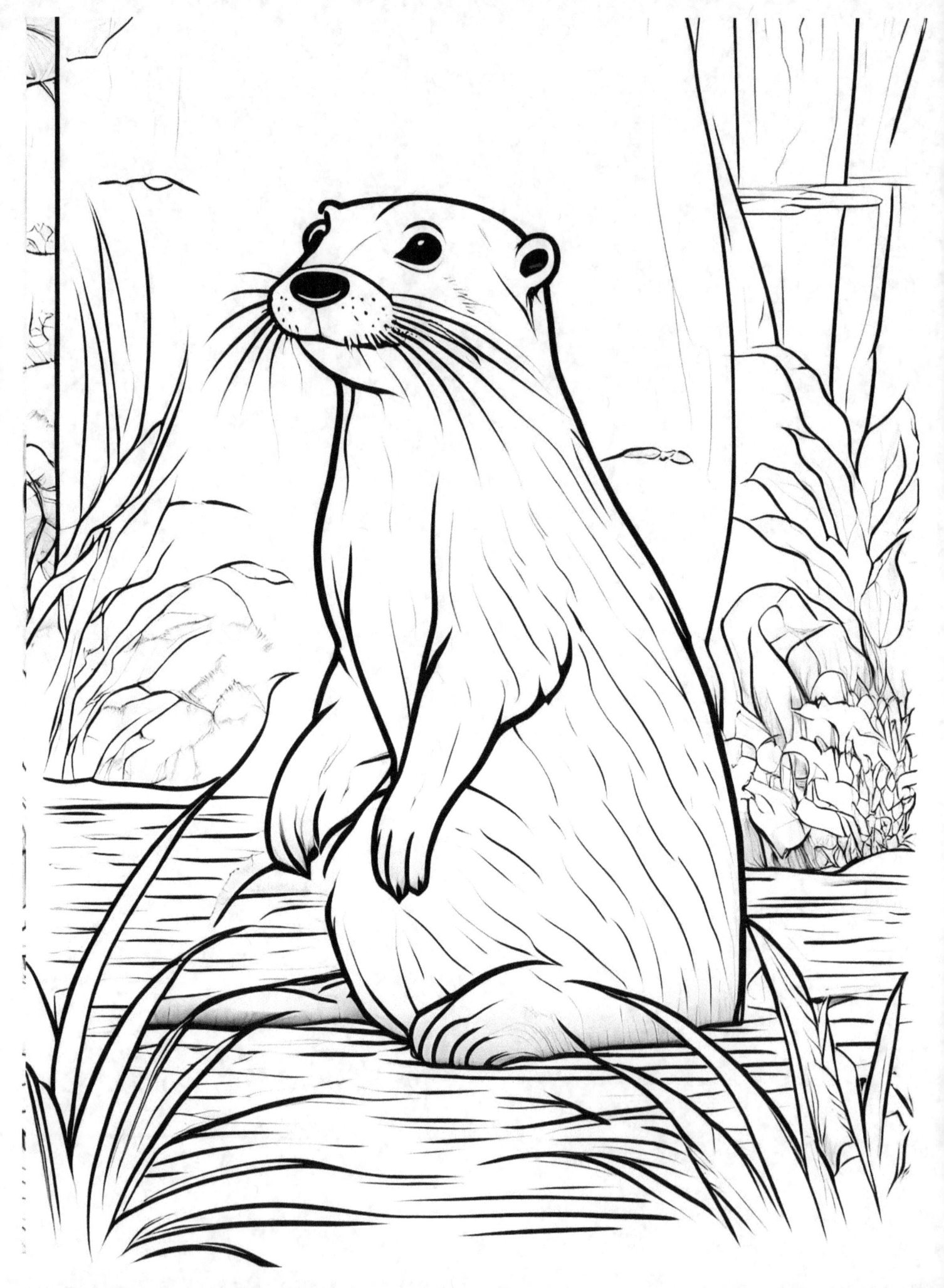

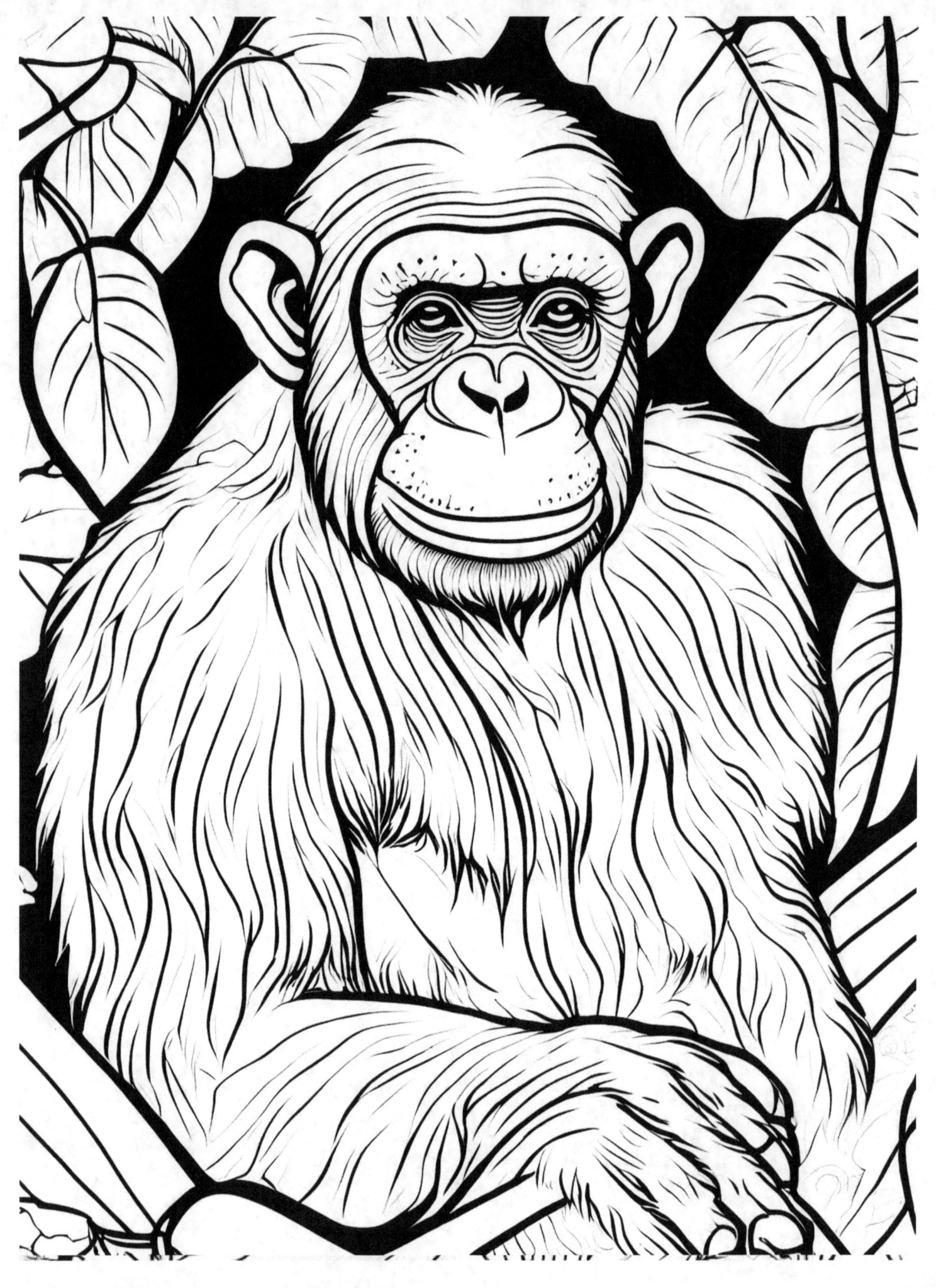

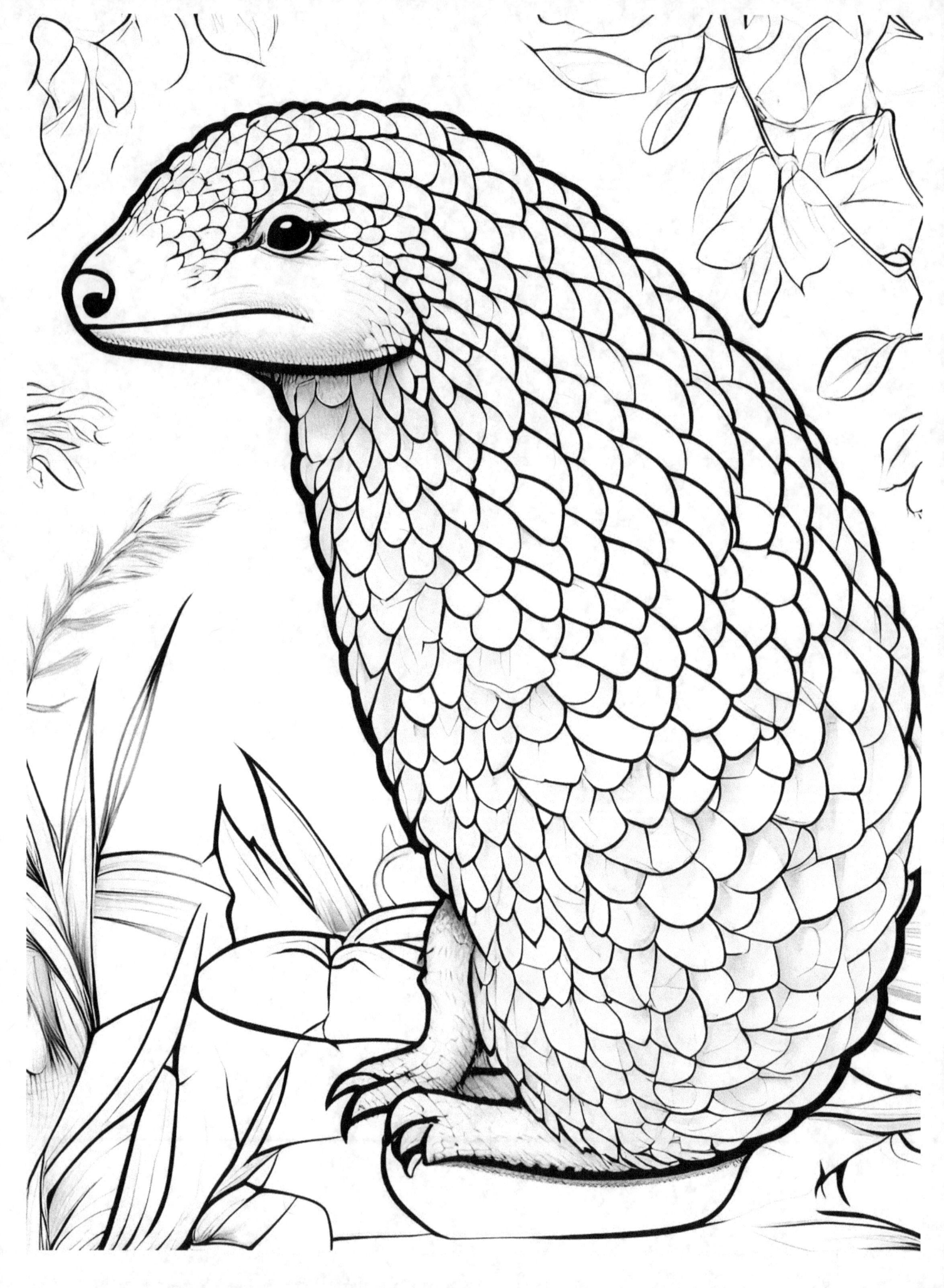

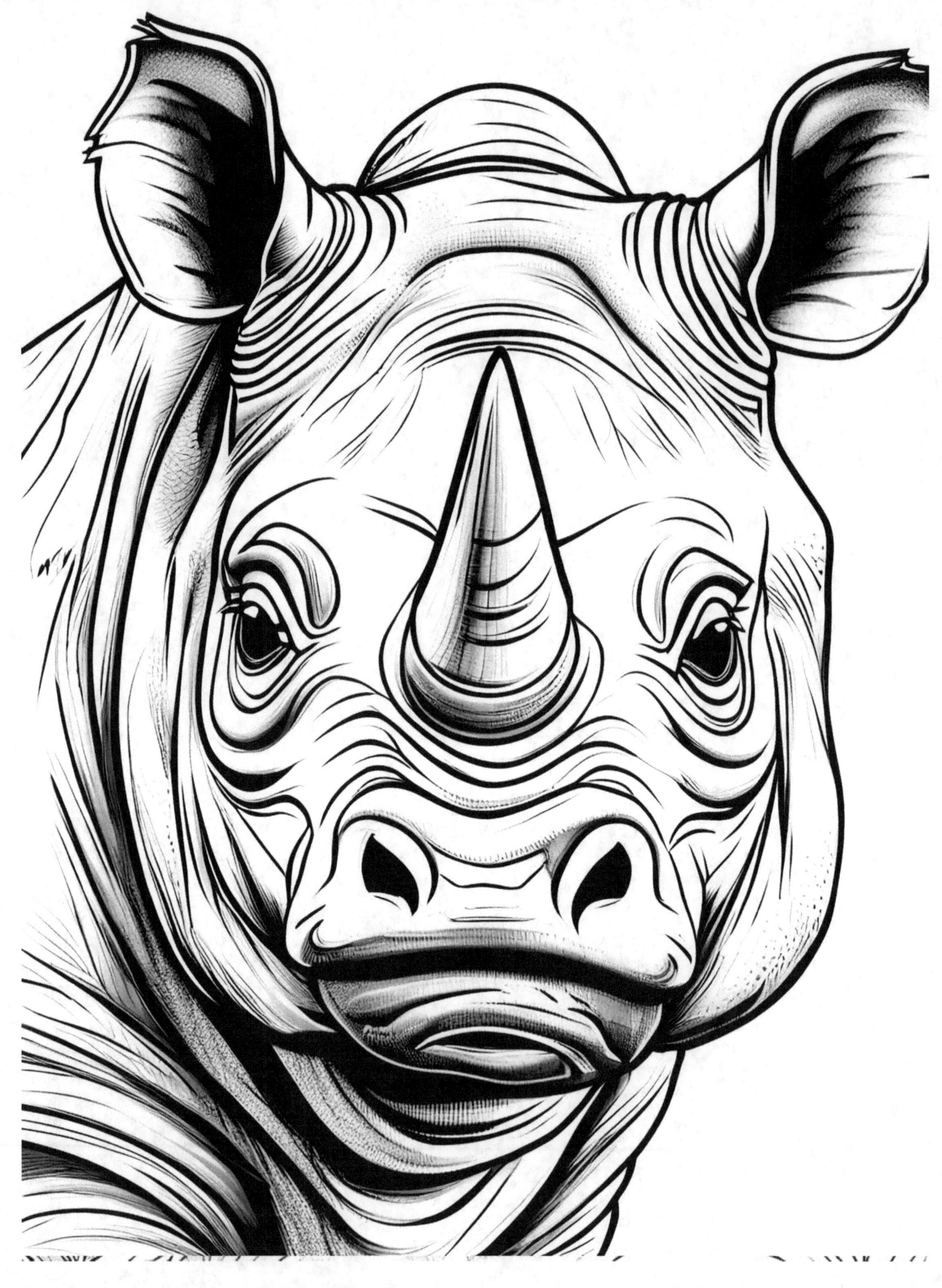

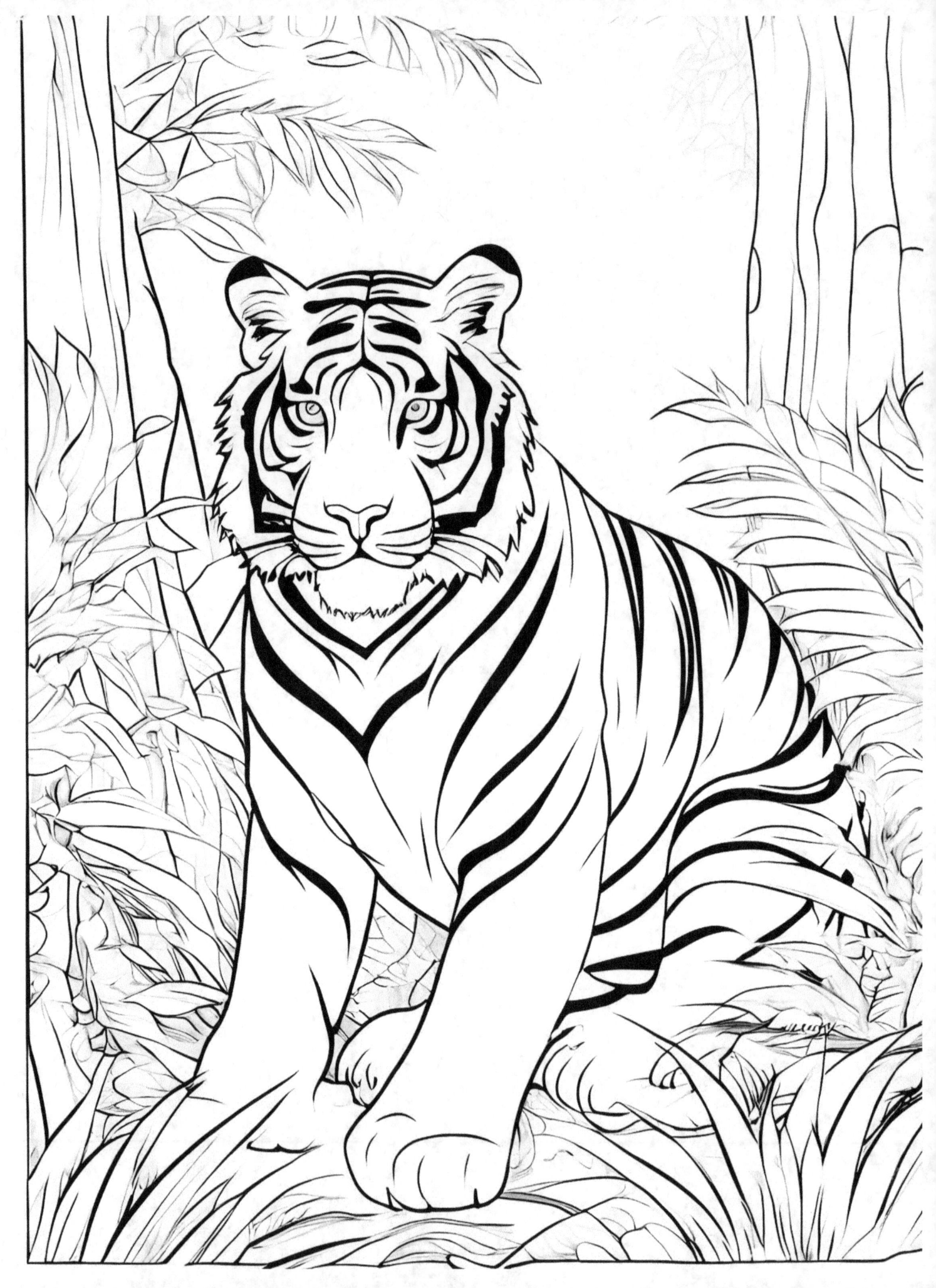

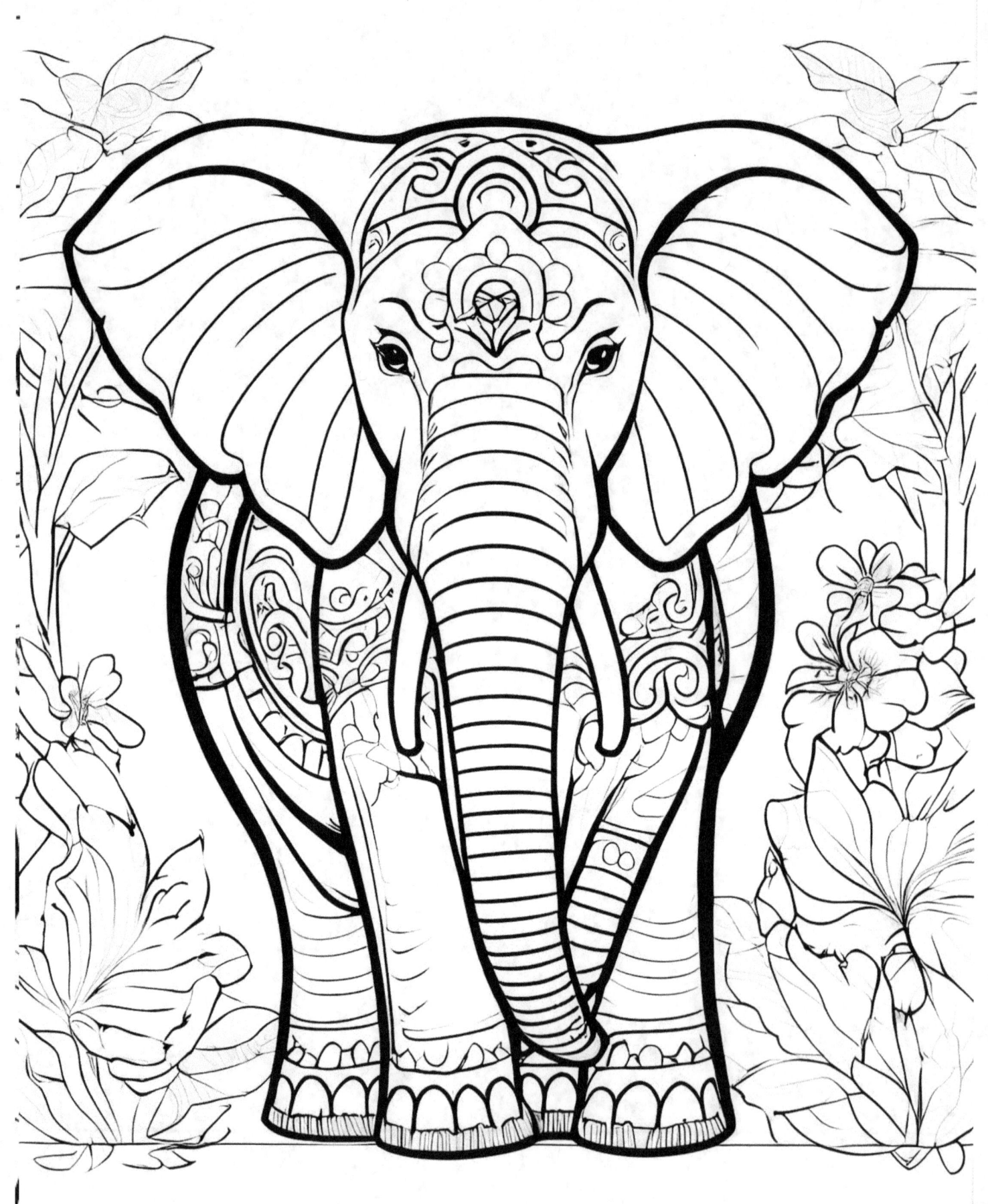

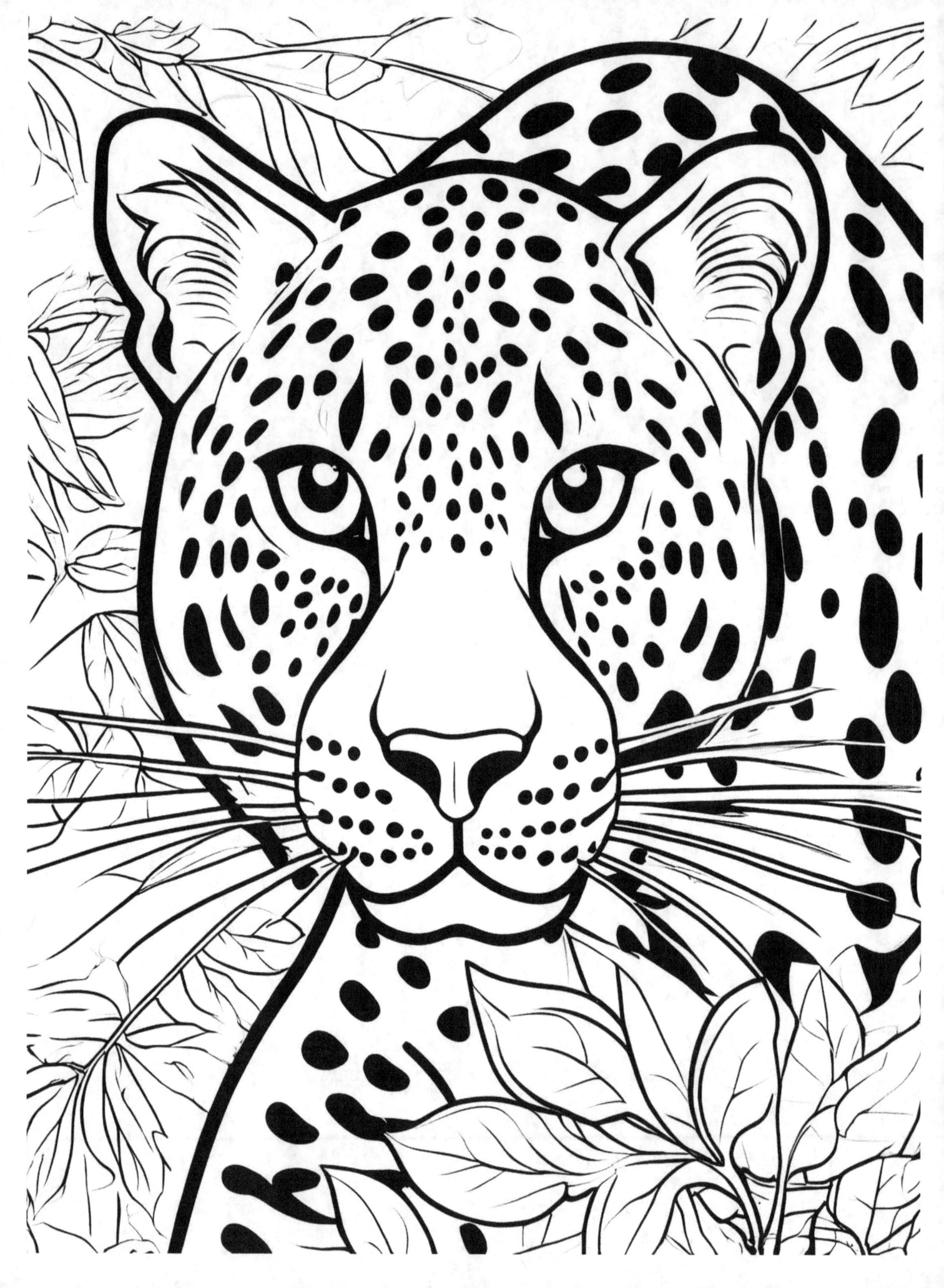

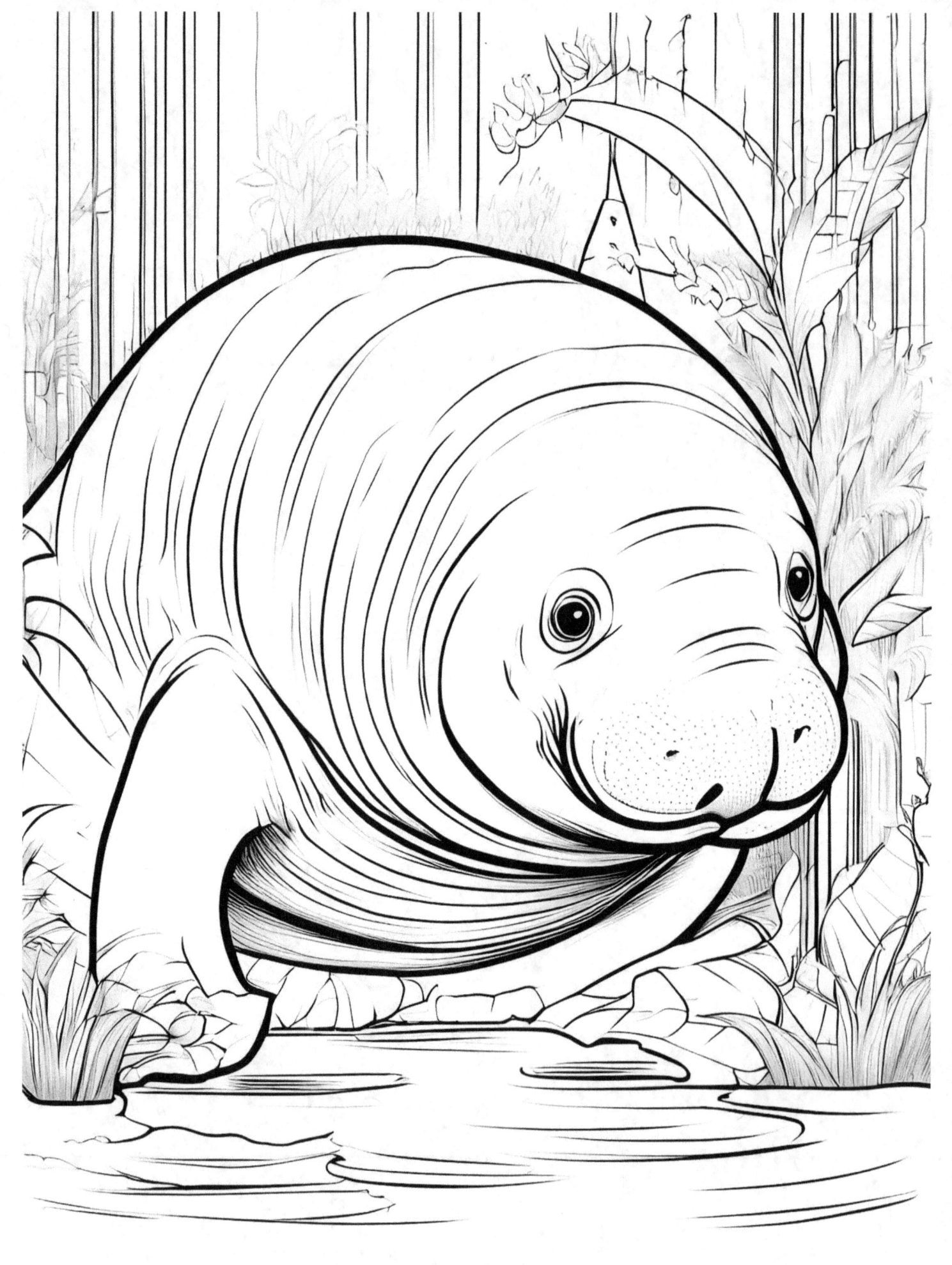

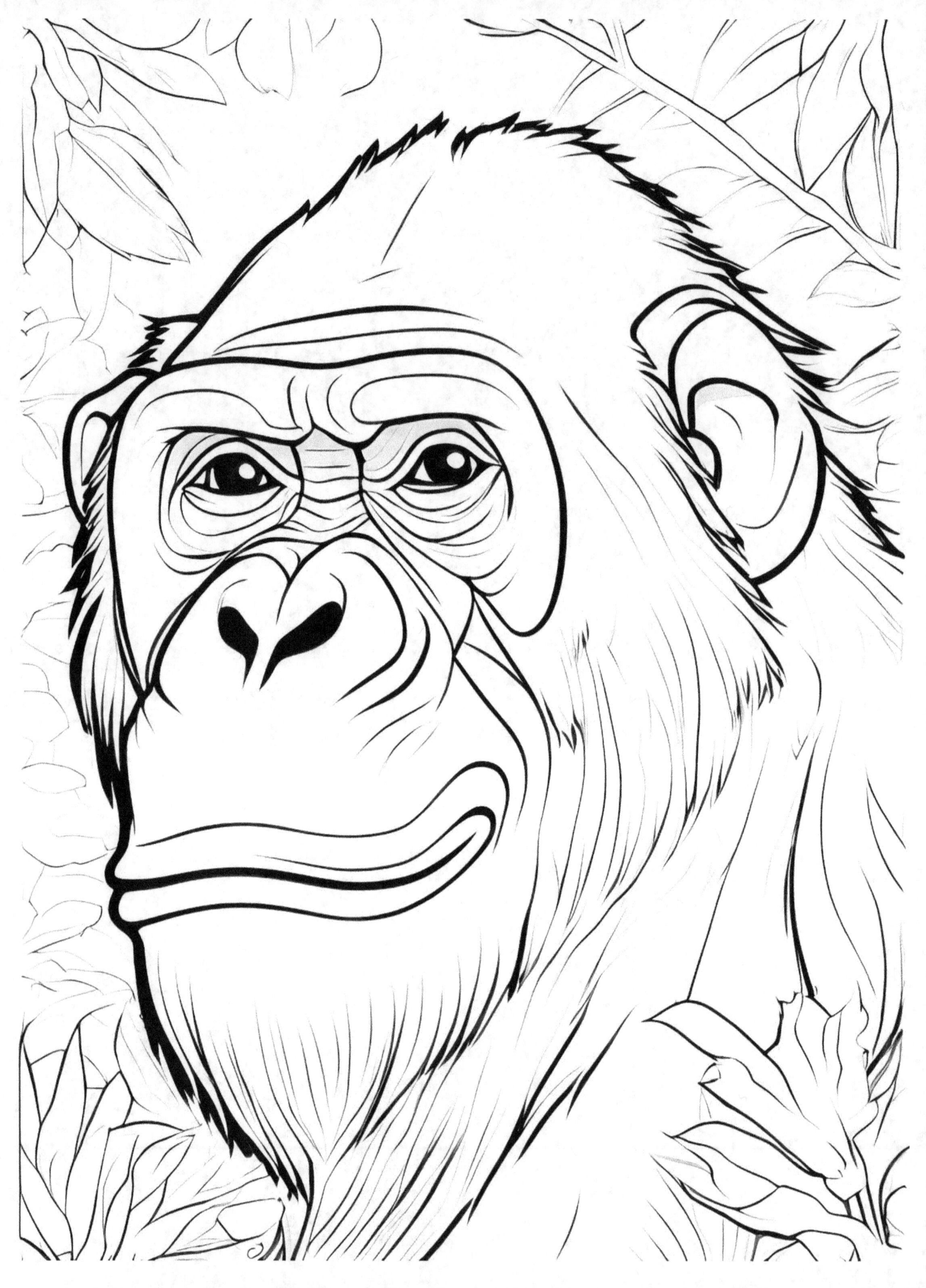

We have reached the end of this lively coloring book, where together we explore the fascinating world of endangered animals. Each page we colored was more than a work of art; it was an act of love and awareness.

As we bring these magnificent animals to life, we also reflect on the importance of preserving their habitats, respecting biodiversity and acting to ensure that they continue to share the planet with us. Every stroke, every color, became a promise that, together, we can make a difference.